WHAT TICKS GOD OFF

The Ways We Irritate God & What We Can Do About It

Bruce Bickel & Stan Jantz

W PUBLISHING GROUP™

www.wpublishinggroup.com

A Division of Thomas Nelson, Inc.
www.ThomasNelson.com

Published by W Publishing Group, a Division of Thomas Nelson, Inc.,
P.O. Box 141000, Nashville, Tennessee, 37214.

ISBN 0-8499-4316-7

Printed in the United States of America
01 02 03 04 05 PHX 9 8 7 6 5 4 3 2 1

CONTENTS

INTRODUCTION

You can fool some of the people all of the time.
And you can fool all of the people some of the time.
But you can't fool God anytime.
And it's what God knows about you that has you worried.

Based on all external appearances, you seem to be a pretty nice person. Of course, we don't know you very well, so we'll assume that you are basically a quality individual except for a few minor faults (which we'll never mention because, hey, what's a slight personality flaw among friends?). But our approval isn't enough, is it? Let's face it: You may be admired by us and the rest of the earth's population, but it's God's opinion of you that counts

As far as your peer group is concerned, you are deemed socially acceptable so long as:

- you have no FBI file,
- your credit history is clean,
- you don't park your car on your front lawn, and
- you don't admit to watching *The Jerry Springer Show*.

In other words, a good person is one who satisfies a certain expectation of common decency. (These universal expectations are lowered considerably for politicians, televangelists, and professional athletes.)

But God evaluates you according to a different standard. First of all, He is holy, so that sets the bar for acceptable behavior rather high. Second, He knows everything; so you can't fool Him with pious behavior on the outside while you contemplate despicable deeds and hold atrocious attitudes on the inside. These two aspects of God's character, when considered in the context of your own thoughts and actions (not the phony ones, but the real ones), lead to a single, inevitable conclusion:

GOD IS PERFECT AND HE KNOWS THAT YOU AREN'T

You don't need us to point out all the ways you've fallen far below God's level of perfection. (We've got enough of our failures to worry about without getting bogged down with yours.) It is enough that *you* know the ways in which you have failed God. We aren't talking about the innocuous, trivial imperfections that God chuckles over, like the time you fell asleep in church and banged your head on the pew in front of you. Nope. We are referring to those things that you do that really tick God off.

Realizing that they have displeased God in a major way, many people are hoping that God is soft on sin. They seek to reinvent Him into a much more jovial and far less holy God. To put it bluntly, they don't want God; they want a celestial Santa Claus. But as you already know (or as you'll soon discover if you have the gumption to keep reading), God is no Santa Claus. While He is a God of love and forgiveness, He is also a God of wrath and righteousness.

It's not nice to make anyone mad at you. But it is really stupid to make the Almighty Creator of the Universe angry. So, if you are a rational-thinking, life-loving person, you ought to be wondering:

- Have you done anything to make God angry?
- Is He ready to dump white-hot burning coals upon your head for something you have done (or didn't do)?
- Is God so mad that you are afraid to walk outside for fear of being struck by lightning? (The newspapers will report it as a freak accident, but you'll know better. Why do you think it's called an "act of God"?)

If you are asking yourself questions like these, then keep reading. This book is for you and anyone else who feels that God has been disappointed and upset over what they've done in their lives. It's also for those folks who believe that they have never done anything that would offend God. Regardless of which category you are in, we've got the same bad news for you:

Bad news:	You have ticked God off in the past.
More bad news:	You are probably still doing it (in ways you don't even realize).
Really bad news:	You don't want God to be mad at you.

But don't despair. It's not all bad news. How about this:

Good news:	You can identify the things you are doing that make God angry.
More good news:	If you change your ways, God isn't going to hold a grudge.
Really good news:	Regardless of what you've done in the past, it is possible to get on God's good side.

We know what you're thinking: As a lawyer (Bruce) and a marketing consultant (Stan), we lack the credentials to write about how you've ticked God off and what you can do about it. Well, you are right about our lack of relevant credentials. (Although, we are sure that lawyers tick God off, so Bruce might have some personal experience there.) That's why we aren't giving you our opinions in the chapters that follow. Instead, we'll give you God's own words, as spoken through the Old Testament prophets.

It was the job of these prophets to proclaim God's principles. Whether they were speaking to the Israelites as a group, or to an individual king, the prophets fearlessly condemned the behavior and attitudes that were repugnant to God, and they warned of God's anger and wrath to come if the people didn't change their ways. For the most part, the prophets were ignored. No, not simply ignored—they were ridiculed. Many Jews simply dismissed them as the lunatic fringe of society. (While we don't want to join in the derision of the prophets, we can understand why the Jews felt this way. Take Ezekiel, for example. His preaching technique was to lie on his side for 390 days and eat only one meal a day cooked over manure.)

As we review the proclamations of twelve different prophets, you'll hear a lot of doom and gloom. That's to be expected when you've ticked God off. But don't let that discourage you. There is hope. While the prophets warned of God's wrath and judgment for thoughts and actions that angered Him, they also preached of God's love and grace. The often-overlooked message of the prophets is God's desire to forgive and to restore a relationship with every person, no matter how badly they have offended Him in the past.

All of us need to hear the message of the Old Testament prophets. It is a message from God Himself:

> Above all, you must understand that no prophecy in Scripture ever came from the prophets themselves or because they wanted to prophesy. It was the Holy Spirit who moved the prophets to speak from God. (2 Peter 1:20–21)

The message of God's anger will shock and distress you. But the message of God's love and forgiveness will inspire and encourage you.

Bruce & Stan

A "MINOR" POINT FROM THE AUTHORS

The last twelve books of the Old Testament are the collected writings of a group of guys commonly referred to as the "Minor Prophets." These were courageous men who proclaimed God's message to an an- tagonistic or apathetic audience. Because God's nature never changes, their message of what ticked God off about three thousand years ago is just as relevant today. And don't let the advent of indoor plumbing, cell phones, and Starbucks fool you. Human nature hasn't changed either, so there are striking and sobering similarities between the attitudes of the Israelites of 1000 B.C. and those of the citizens of the twenty-first century.

We feel a little sorry for the Minor Prophets because they don't get the recognition of the four so-called "Major Prophets." First of all, the roster of the Minor Prophets doesn't include any names with marquee value, like Daniel and those other heavy hitters—Ezekiel, Jeremiah, and Isaiah. The Minor Prophets, on the other hand, have been relegated to obscurity because their names are much harder to pronounce. Really. Go to the maternity ward in any hospital. You're bound to find a few Daniels and even a Jeremiah or two. But the odds are astronomical against finding even one Habakkuk.

But the real slam against the Minor Prophets is the fact that they are referred to as *minor*. The whole *major* versus *minor* distinction brings to mind the tier system in professional baseball. People immediately assume that the Major Prophets are the pros, and the Minor Prophets just couldn't make the cut into the big leagues. Well, it isn't that way at all. The distinction between the Major and Minor Prophets has nothing to do with the quality of their messages and everything to do with the length of the books they wrote. The Major Prophets were much more long-winded, and each of their books consumed an entire scroll. But the writings of all twelve of the Minor Prophets could be contained on a single scroll. So don't let that unfortunate, disparaging terminology throw you off. The Minor Prophets still pack a major message.

We'll present the message of the twelve Minor Prophets in the order in which they appear in your Bible. That order is not chronological (it's not even alphabetically arranged), so you might find a quick-read summary of the historical context to be helpful.

During the reign of David (the slingshot shepherd boy who became king), the nation of Israel flexed its military muscle and expanded its territory. After King David's death, the throne was occupied by his son, Solomon (a *real* wise guy), and Israel experienced its greatest prosperity.

But civil war broke out after Solomon died, and the nation of Israel was divided into two separate countries. The northern country, representing ten of the original Hebrew tribes, retained the rights to the name *Israel*. The country in the south, referred to as *Judah*, represented the other two tribes. The capital city of Jerusalem was in Judah.

For the most part, incompetent kings ruled the northern nation of Israel. Despite the warnings of the prophets, the nation strayed far away from God as it formed alliances with its pagan neighbors. As punishment, and as a means of bringing His people back to Himself, God allowed the northern nation of Israel to be invaded and captured by the Assyrians in 722 B.C.

The southern kingdom of Judah had a better set of kings, and it maintained a modicum of allegiance to God. In response to the preaching of some of the prophets, Judah would at times turn back to God. While Judah survived the threats and attacks of the Assyrians, it suffered invasion and capture by the Babylonians in 586 B.C.

Many of the Jews from the northern country of Israel were dispersed within the Assyrian territory. When the Babylonians conquered the Assyrian Empire and then invaded Judah, captives from Jerusalem were exiled in Babylon. The great city of Jerusalem was in ruins, and the regions of Israel and Judah were desolate. This time span (from about 586 to 536 B.C.) is referred to as the Babylonian Exile Period.

The Postexilic Period (beginning in 536 B.C.) marked the start of the return of Jews to their home country and the rebuilding of the city of Jerusalem.

As we present the message of the Minor Prophets in the pages that follow, we'll keep giving you the historical context. But we think you'll be surprised that the passage of several thousand years doesn't alter the behavior of humanity or the nature of God.

1

LOOKING FOR LOVE
IN ALL THE WRONG PLACES

There has been quite a transformation in television over the past several decades. We aren't talking about the progression from black-and-white, to color, to HDTV. We are referring to content. In its infancy and adolescence, television consisted of shows within the comfortable and predictable confines of traditional society. Now, having come of age, television seeks to explore the boundaries and push the edges of societal behavior. We said good-bye to Ed Sullivan because accordion players, plate spinners, and ventriloquists were no longer a "really big show." Instead, people tune in to watch Howard Stern and Jerry Springer and their parade of perverts.

The shift in societal "norms" is perhaps best illustrated by television's portrayal of love and marriage. There was a time, not too long ago, when TV marriages were characterized by commitment and fidelity. Whether you were watching Lucy and Desi, Ozzie and Harriet, or Ward and June Cleaver, you never wondered if one spouse was going to cheat on the other. But then came the couples on *Dallas* and *Dynasty,* where infidelity occurred as frequently as the commercials.

We can still find a few shows on television in which faithfulness in marriage exists, but you have to be watching Nick at Night to see most of them. The current trend in programming, however, seems to promote infidelity. The settings of these so-called "reality" shows vary slightly, but they share a common element. Whether it's an island, a cruise ship, or a backyard hot tub, the environment is always conducive to swimwear (ranging from surfer shorts to dental-floss thongs). The gimmick is to test the level of a couple's fidelity against the distractions and temptations of "competitors" who are flexing their pecs or bouncing their bosoms.

Let's face it. In our culture, marital infidelity has lost its stigma, and fidelity has lost its nobility. Infidelity is portrayed so often on television that we are no longer shocked or surprised when it happens in real life. With every occurrence—whether with politicians, ministers, or our neighbors—we become a little more used to it.

So what's our point? Are we beginning this book by saying that God is ticked off by raunchy TV shows that denigrate the sanctity of marriage? No, that isn't what we are getting at. Oh, we are sure that much of what is broadcast on the airwaves is repulsive to Him, but God might like a few of the current programs. (We tell our wives that *Monday Night Football* is one of His favorites.) Television is not the problem—infidelity is. But not the kind you may be thinking about.

GOD IS TICKED OFF BY OUR INFIDELITY TOWARD HIM

Would you be hurt, offended, and outraged if your spouse cheated on you? Of course! Well, God has similar emotions when we are unfaithful and let our affections wander away from Him.

It is terrible that our society has become accustomed to marital infidelity, but it is even more tragic that Christians have become oblivious to their own spiritual infidelity. God won't put up with it for long. If we don't turn back to Him on our own, He may bring circumstances upon us that will force us to reconsider.

Spiritual infidelity is nothing new. Throughout human history, God has been jilted and His love has been spurned. When it happened with the nation of Israel eight centuries before the birth of Christ, God used the prophet Hosea to confront the Jews with their unfaithfulness. But it wasn't enough for Hosea to just pontificate about God's sorrow, pain, and anger. To ensure that Hosea understood how God grieved over Israel's spiritual adultery, God put Hosea in a prime-time reality show that had all of Israel talking.

In Love with a Philandering Gomer

The time was about 750 B.C. The place was the northern country of Israel. The nation of Israel was at its pinnacle in terms of prosperity and power. In its quest for wealth and political alliances, Israel had adopted the cultural practices of its pagan neighbors. God commissioned Hosea to warn the nation of Israel that it was guilty of spiritual adultery because it had turned away from God. God's judgment was going to fall on Israel for its unfaithfulness, but Hosea wanted to assure the nation that the coming hardship (invasion by the Assyrians) was a form of discipline designed to bring Israel back to Him.

Some of the best sermons are the ones preached from personal experience. Since Hosea had a tough message to preach, and an audience that didn't care to hear it, God put Hosea through a life experience that caught the attention of the nation and made Hosea passionate about the message.

Prophets with a Flair for the Dramatic

The prophets of the Old Testament usually delivered God's message by conventional means: the spoken and the written word. But that wasn't always the case. Sometimes it was delivered with a bit of symbolic theatrics for added emphasis:

- Ahijah ripped his cloak into twelve pieces to visually demonstrate that Solomon's empire would be divided by civil war (1 Kings 11:29–40).
- Jeremiah smashed pottery to illustrate how God was going to bring destruction to Jerusalem as punishment for the sin of its citizens (Jeremiah 19:1–13).
- Isaiah walked around naked for three years to show Judah the shame and humiliation (and chafing) it would experience from its captors (Isaiah 20:1–5).

A three-year stint of public nudity on the dusty streets of Jerusalem is a tough assignment for a prophet. But Isaiah didn't mind. He probably knew what God was putting Hosea through in order to bring a real-life illustration to Hosea's preaching. Compared to Hosea's humiliation, Isaiah's nudity was a breeze (pun intended).

A Babe by Any Other Name Would Look the Same

The story of Hosea begins with him as a bachelor. Like all the other guys his age, he was anxious to find a nice Jewish girl to marry. The singles' scene in Israel wasn't all that great, and Hosea was probably dreading the fact that he would be stuck in a marriage arranged by his parents. After all, he was just a poor, itinerant prophet, and the prospects for the kind of woman he could afford to marry weren't too exciting.

Although he might have been dreading an arranged marriage, Hosea hadn't counted on God doing the arranging. Imagine his delight when God told Hosea that the most beautiful woman in all of Israel had been chosen for his wife. There were, however, two slight drawbacks:

- First, her name was *Gomer*. (Whispering that name in the midst of a passionate embrace would undoubtedly spoil the moment, so we're sure that Hosea called Gomer by some sort of nickname—like *Monique*.)
- Second, God told Hosea that Gomer was going to be unfaithful to him. (OK, so maybe this wasn't exactly a *slight* drawback.) And there was more bad news. They would have children, but some of those kids would be fathered by Gomer's other lovers.

As Hosea wondered whether God had slipped off His celestial rocker, God explained:

> This will illustrate the way my people have been untrue to me, openly committing adultery against the LORD by worshiping other gods. (Hosea 1:2)

So Hosea did as God instructed him, and the entire town turned out to celebrate the nuptials of Hosea and Gomer. Despite all that God had told him about the future, Hosea loved Gomer with all of his heart. He was entirely devoted to her.

Extra, Extramarital Affairs

The marriage apparently thrived at first. The loving couple was pleased to announce the birth of their first child, a son. A daughter and another son followed quickly, but rumors started to swirl about whether or not Hosea was the father of the second and third children. If Hosea had any hopes that his love for Gomer could keep her faithful to him, God squelched such hopes by telling Hosea the names that should be given to each of his children. Here are their Hebrew names, with a loosely translated English meaning:

- For their first child, God chose the name *Jezreel*, meaning "castaway," which was a shameful term in Israel.
- It didn't get any better for Hosea's daughter, whom God named *Lo-ruhamah*, which means, "not loved."
- You can understand why the neighbors questioned the third child's parentage when God called him *Lo-ammi*, meaning "not my people."

It had to be tough on Hosea when people started to gossip about Gomer's promiscuity. But it had to be even harder when he introduced someone to his family: "And I'd like you to meet my wife, Gomer. (Gomer, please cover up your cleavage.) And these are my three children: Castaway, Not Loved, and Not My People."

It is said that marriages are made in heaven. Well, so are thunderstorms and lightning. It wasn't too long before this marriage made in heaven got very stormy. Gomer started running around with other men. She wasn't even discreet about it. Throughout Israel and Judah the tale of "The Prophet and the Prostitute" was told.

With each sexual affair, Gomer's beauty faded. She became used merchandise, and each successive lover was more abusive than the last. But Hosea's love for his wife never faded. He watched out for her welfare even when she would not return to him. Some scholars believe that Hosea would go to the man she was then living with and give him food, clothes, and money for her. She never stopped to consider where these unexpected provisions came from; she probably gave credit to the same creep who had beaten her earlier in the evening.

Gomer's life was in a death spiral. She hit bottom when one of her sexual partners put her up for sale on the slave market. But as he had always done in the past, Hosea came to the rescue. He paid the purchase price for his wife. (It wasn't much. She went for the marked-down price of a crippled slave.) He took her back to their home, and he reiterated his pledge of unconditional love to her. Gomer was amazed by his display of ardent and sincere affection and the forgiveness he extended to her. Her rebellious and wayward heart was broken. She accepted his love and abandoned her immorality, and their marriage was restored.

The Adultery Analogy

The analogy between Gomer and Israel was painfully obvious to Hosea. The grief that he suffered as the result of Gomer's unrestrained immorality was just a fraction of the sorrow that God felt over the spiritual infidelity of Israel. Hosea had endured a marriage of one-sided love and faithfulness, exactly as God had with the adulterous Israel.

The Israelites loved to gossip about Gomer's extramarital affairs, but they refused to acknowledge that their relationship with God was similar in any fashion. If they had only taken the time to briefly review their own history, the nature of their spiritual infidelity would have been blatantly apparent.

God's original covenant with the patriarch Abraham included the covenant of a promised land for his descendants, premised on the condition that the Israelites rid that geographic region of the corrupt civilizations that occupied it. God did not want His children to be influenced by pagan cultures. From the time the children of Israel entered the Promised Land under the military leadership of Joshua, through the reign of King David, they never did completely rid their land of the heathen influences. For similar reasons, Hebrew laws discouraged intermarriage with foreigners. This had nothing to do with discrimination on the basis of ethnicity. It was simply to avoid compromising their beliefs in God with pagan influences.

But the Israelites did not rid their land of the corrupt Canaanites. And they did not insulate themselves against pagan influences. Quite the contrary. The Israelites actually absorbed the Canaanite rituals and pagan practices into their own lifestyle. Just as Gomer left Hosea and crawled into bed with another man, so the Israelites left their first love for the worship of lesser gods.

The Canaanites had a culture, that centered on the worship of idols. They had a god for everything, the most important of whom was *Baal* (a name used to describe all of the lesser gods as well). The Canaanites believed that Baal was responsible for agricultural production. Since they wanted to eat, they wanted to keep Baal happy. They believed that Baal was male, and that he had a female consort called *Astarte*. The fertility of the land was determined by the sexual activity of Baal and Astarte. To encourage Baal's sexual appetite, the Canaanites performed cult prostitution, orgies, and other erotic practices at the temples and shrines as an integral part of their worship.

Little by little, the Israelites got caught up in the worship of Baal. By the time Hosea came on the scene, the beliefs and practices of Canaanite culture had been adopted and absorbed into the worship of the Lord by the Israelites. They even worshiped God in shrines and temples for Baal, along with religious celebrations that included drunkenness and debauchery. Sexual adultery and spiritual adultery were, in fact, closely linked in Hosea's time, because idolatry and sexual promiscuity were linked in practice. The Israelites' love and worship of God had been defiled.

Through Hosea, God identified the ways in which the nation of Israel had been unfaithful to Him. Importantly, God's definition of spiritual adultery was not limited to activities that involved pagan rituals of sexual excess and idol worship. Hosea also proclaimed that Israel's infidelity took the following forms:

- Failing to acknowledge that God was the source of her prosperity and wealth (Hosea 2:2–13)
- Ignoring or forgetting God (13:4–6)
- Abandoning God's laws and any connection between Him and the routine of real life (4:1–2)
- Arrogance toward God and rebellion against His precepts (7:10 and 13:6)
- Spiritual hypocrisy (6:4–6)

Although they professed loyalty to God, they were just going through the motions of religious rituals. Like "the morning mist," the significance of their acts evaporated easily and had no real meaning or substance (6:4). At the root of the spiritual adultery were the unfaithfulness of their idolatry and the unfaithfulness of their immorality. But it didn't stop there. God declared that their infidelity extended to the actions that resulted from the compromises of their faith: social injustice (12:7); violent crime (4:2, 6:9, 12:1); political revolt (7:6–7); foreign alliances (7:11, 8:9); and spiritual ingratitude (7:15).

Gomer had prostituted herself for the empty love of other men. Israel had prostituted herself for a lifestyle of self-gratification. Gomer's physical adultery was a picture of Israel's spiritual adultery. It was not a pretty picture.

Israel in the Gutter

When Hosea began preaching, the nation of Israel was prosperous and growing, or so it appeared on the outside. Internally, however, its moral corruption and spiritual adultery were eating away at the fabric of the nation. Hosea's message was ignored at first because Israel was arrogantly absorbed in its "glamour age." But there was nothing glamorous about it, because it was really a time of moral and spiritual decay.

Within three decades of the start of Hosea's ministry, Israel began to suffer the toll of ignoring God. Just as Gomer had taken a nosedive, the prosperity of Israel came to an abrupt stop. Before it knew what had happened, it was being sold on the slave market.

The downfall of Israel shouldn't have been a surprise to anyone. Hosea had predicted that God was going to bring His discipline upon Israel for its unfaithfulness. And that's exactly what happened: Israel suffered twin judgments of increased violence and environmental crisis (as predicted in Hosea 4:1–3), and if that wasn't enough, Assyria invaded and destroyed Israel in 722 B.C. (as prophesied in Hosea 4:19).

But God's Love Continues

Some analogies fall apart if you try to stretch them too far. But the story of Hosea and Gomer is a complete analogy of God's love for Israel in all respects. Don't forget how the story of Hosea and Gomer ended. Even after Gomer's decadent lifestyle and complete rejection of his love, Hosea's love for her knew no limits. He went to great lengths to restore the marriage, even to the point of purchasing Gomer at the slave market. And so it is with God's love for Israel.

Each judgment that God brought upon Israel was premised in discipline. Because of His love for His people, God brought circumstances into their lives that caused them to return to Him. Like Gomer, when they had nowhere else to go, they turned back to God. That was the intent of it all. And God never left or abandoned Israel.

Hosea never forgot about the day when he rescued Gomer and brought her home and restored their marriage. He probably had that picture in his mind when he preached these words to Israel:

> Return, O Israel, to the LORD your God, for your sins have brought you down. Bring your petitions, and return to the LORD. Say to him, "Forgive all our sins and graciously receive us, so that we may offer you the sacrifice of praise. . . . The LORD says, "Then I will heal you of your idolatry and faithlessness, and my love will know no bounds, for my anger will be gone forever!" (14:1–2, 4)

God's love is not a conditional love; it is an open-hearted, generous self-giving which God offers to men. Those who would carefully limit the operation of God's love . . . have missed the point.

—J.B. Phillips

Spiritual Adultery? Who, Me?

As we see it, there are at least three important aspects to Hosea's story:

- First and foremost, we learn about the faithfulness of God despite the faithlessness of His people.
- Second and equally obvious, we learn that God is ticked off when the people He loves are guilty of spiritual infidelity.
- But third, and perhaps most regrettably, we discover that *we* are guilty of the same type of spiritual adultery that was

committed by Israel. (That "we" means Bruce and Stan, but it also includes *you*.)

If you are a bit defensive, you might reply, "I've never committed spiritual adultery. Not once have I danced naked on the altar to the god Baal." Well, we are thankful for that, but remember that the essence of Israel's spiritual infidelity was the abandonment of God's precepts and the adoption of the habits and lifestyle of a godless culture. If we are honest with ourselves, we are certainly guilty of that.

Most of us are deeply entrenched in the customs of our culture. Although it happens unintentionally, we pick up the habits and lifestyles of people who have no love for God. We let their attitudes and actions have too much influence on us (instead of the other way around). We drift their way instead of attracting them to God. That's exactly what the Israelites did, and that's exactly what ticked God off.

Maybe Gomer didn't realize the danger of her unfaithfulness when she had that first drink with a stranger at the neighborhood oasis. But that was the beginning of her infidelity. Our spiritual adultery may also appear harmless at first. But after a while, we get caught up in the culture and lose our appreciation, respect, and devotion to God. We get farther away and our hearts become calloused toward Him. Then we pursue ambitions that do not include Him. The next sin becomes easier to commit. And the next. As we continue to compromise God's principles, we can get to the point at which we are completely unfaithful to God.

Just as Gomer's relationship with Hosea was ruined by an accelerating downward spiral of immorality, we jeopardize our relationships with God as we are more and more enticed by the selfish pleasures of our culture. The downward spiral is very predictable:

Stage 1: Your focus on God is *distracted* by something that appeals to you. You know you shouldn't allow your attention to be taken away from God, but it seems harmless (and you'll only do it for a moment).

Stage 2: Your energies are *diverted* away from God. You spend your time and resources on something that actually interferes with the relationship between you and God.

Stage 3: You might not intend to offend God, but your actions reveal an intentional rebellion against Him. You might be able to maintain a facade of spirituality, but your relationship with God has *deteriorated* due to your defiance.

Stage 4: For a while, Gomer would sneak out of the house to meet with other men. But then there came a point when she had not even a shred of feeling for Hosea. She moved out. She *deserted* him entirely. That's the final stage that occurs if you continue to give your affections to other people and things instead of to God.

The Israelites had Hosea to confront them with the nature and extent of their spiritual adultery. Who do we have? Well, the message of Hosea remains applicable today. We are unfaithful to God when:

- we fail to acknowledge that God is the source of our prosperity and wealth (2:2–13),
- we ignore or forget God (13:4–6),
- we abandon God's laws and any connection between Him and the routine of real life (Hosea 4:1–2),
- we act arrogantly toward God and rebel against His precepts (7:10 and 13:6), and
- we fake a level of Christianity that boils down to nothing more than spiritual hypocrisy (6:4–6).

When viewed in this context, our spiritual adultery is as obvious as Gomer's physical adultery. We can see it in how we handle our finances, when we fail to acknowledge His provision and consider ourselves self-sufficient just because we have a high-powered job or a fat IRA. We ignore Him when we squander our wealth without any sense of stewardship. Like Israel, we spend without respecting the Source and Provider of our wealth.

And we can see our faithlessness when we have too much fun with the pleasures of life to carve out any time for God. Of course, we don't say it like that. Instead, we put a spiritual spin on it: "I want to read the Bible and pray, but my schedule is just too busy." But we don't fool God. He knows that in the back of our minds we are thinking: "The spirit is willing, but my flesh is anxious to party."

Hosea's message helps us identify the problem of our spiritual adultery: It is anything that captures our affections, attention and priorities. Such behavior ticks God off, so we shouldn't be surprised if He allows hardship into our lives. Maybe we need to land in the gutter so the only place to look is up. But maybe not. Maybe we can use the message of Hosea as a warning before it is too late. Hosea encourages us to return to our first love. We know that God is anxious to have us love Him back.

The life story of Hosea symbolizes the forgiving and faithful nature of God: He is faithful to us even though we are unfaithful to Him. We have been guilty of spiritual infidelity, but if we repent and return to God, He will take us back.

Apologies for Spiritual Adultery

Don't believe the platitude that "love means never having to say you're sorry." It is false. True love involves repentance. And repentance is what Hosea says is the first step in restoring our relationship with God. (See the quote from Hosea 14 on page 9.)

Most of us aren't very articulate when it comes to asking God for forgiveness and repenting of our sins. But Pastor Joe Wright doesn't have such a problem. Pastor Wright lives in Kansas, and he was asked to open a session of the Kansas Senate with a prayer. There was nothing unusual about the request. Many legislative sessions are opened with a token prayer. The Kansas Senate was simply following the common practice of asking local clergy members to invoke a divine blessing on the daily proceedings. Everybody was expecting a typical glib, cursory, generic prayer on the day Pastor Wright was scheduled to pray. What they heard, however, was a heartfelt, impassioned prayer of repentance for the spiritual adultery of our society. It is reported that his prayer went like this:

> Heavenly Father, we come before you today to ask your forgiveness and to seek your direction and guidance. We know Your Word says, "Woe to those who call evil good," but that is exactly what we have done. We have lost our spiritual equilibrium and reversed our values. We confess that.

We have ridiculed the absolute truth of Your Word and called it pluralism. We have exploited the poor and called it the lottery. We have rewarded laziness and called it welfare. We have killed our unborn and called it choice. We have shot abortionists and called it justifiable. We have neglected to discipline our children and called it building self-esteem. We have abused power and called it politics. We have coveted our neighbor's possessions and called it ambition. We have polluted the air with profanity and pornography and called it freedom of expression. We have ridiculed the time-honored values of our forefathers and called it enlightenment.

Search us, O God, and know our hearts today. Cleanse us from every sin and set us free. Amen.

A number of legislators gave Reverend Wright the same treatment the Israelites gave to Hosea. They walked out on him. But that prayer struck a responsive chord with the citizens of Kansas and others around the world. Within six weeks after offering that prayer, Pastor Wright's church received more than five thousand calls, with only forty-seven of them critical of what he had said. Radio commentator Paul Harvey featured this prayer on *The Rest of the Story*, and that single program has elicited more responses than Harvey has ever received to any of his other broadcasts.

The response to Pastor Wright's prayer is encouraging. Maybe the message of Hosea is getting through to us. Maybe it's not too late. Maybe we haven't gone so far that our hearts have been hardened to God's love. Maybe we can turn from our unfaithfulness and return to God. Let's give Him the love, worship, and priority that He deserves. Instead of loving what the world has to offer, let's love God.

> Stop loving this evil world and all that it offers you, for when you love the world, you show that you do not have the love of the Father in you. For the world offers only the lust for physical pleasure, the lust for everything we see, and pride in our possessions. These are not from the Father. They are from this evil world. And this world is fading away, along with everything it craves. But if you do the will of God, you will live forever. (1 John 2:15–17)

IT'S NEVER TOO LATE TO TURN BACK

People are fascinated with natural disasters—unless, of course, the disaster is happening to them. As long as we're sitting comfortably in our living rooms watching Fox, we get a certain visceral charge when viewing *The World's Greatest Natural Disasters*. There's something about nature run amok that widens our eyes.

Don't worry if you haven't been watching the Fox disaster specials. We know you're interested, so we have compiled for you the most famous natural disasters on American soil over the last hundred years or so. We have selected disasters from three different categories: earthquakes, hurricanes, and volcanic eruptions. These are natural phenomena that occur on a really big scale.

- The most famous earthquake we could think of occurred in San Francisco in 1906. This 7.9 Richter-scale jolt and the fires it spawned killed 3,000 people and destroyed 28,000 buildings.
- The costliest hurricane in U.S. history was Hurricane Andrew, which engulfed the southern part of Florida in 1992, killing 41 people and causing $17.5 billion in damage.
- The most spectacular volcanic eruption occurred on Mount St. Helens in Washington in 1980. The blast blew off the top 1,300 feet of the mountain, sent gases and ash as high as 12 miles, and killed 57 people.

As much as we'd like to think that everything big happens in America, our natural disasters pale in comparison to disasters worldwide. In 1976 an earthquake in Tangshan, China killed a quarter million people. Half a million people died in Bangladesh in 1970 as a result of a cyclone. And the famous Krakatoa volcano in southwestern Indonesia killed thirty-six thousand people when it erupted in 1883.

If you think the earth has been relatively quiet lately, you haven't been keeping up with current events. According to the experts, the world was hit by 850 natural disasters in 2000, more than any other year in history. And the people who keep track of this stuff say that future years are likely to be even worse. We can expect disastrous floods and famine to hit different parts of the world at the same time. Earthquakes and tidal waves will decimate vast regions and likely kill hundreds of thousands of people.

So what's going on? Is the earth really upset over some things we've done, or are there other forces at work? We've always had this nice, cozy live-and-let-live relationship with Planet Earth, but things seem to be getting rather nasty lately. One minute she's showing off her beauty and wonder, and the next thing we know she's ripping us apart.

All of which begs the question: How can all of these destructive things happen in a world created by a perfect and loving God? Has God lost control of the world He made? Have things gotten so out of whack that even God is unable or unwilling to prevent big-time disasters? Or does He cause them, making Him responsible for the terrible things happening in our world, including the deaths of millions of people. Some people even go so far as to say that God causes—or at least allows—natural disasters for one simple reason:

GOD IS TICKED OFF BY OUR SIN

Now, few would argue that sin ticks God off (we're going to talk more about that in a minute). But is God so mad that He's using the forces of nature to punish us, or at least get our attention? Whether or not you agree with that idea (and we're not sure that we do), we need to look at God and nature. More specifically, we need to look at whether God is in control of nature, or if nature acts on its own, without His involvement.

As we're going to see in this chapter, no matter how random and unpredictable natural disasters seem, God is in total control. Not only did He create the universe and everything in it (Genesis 1:1), but He also keeps it going (Colossians 1:16–17). Nothing happens—including the destructive forces of the savage earth (as PBS called it)—unless God allows it. In every way, shape, and form, God is the master of the universe. He rules every galaxy, every planet, and every living being, down to the smallest particle.

So if God is in control, and He allows destruction to take place, does that mean He is also responsible for it? In a word, yes. If God is in control, then He is responsible. If that's hard to believe and even harder to accept, consider the alternative: If God isn't responsible, then He isn't in control, and nature works under its own power, or worse, under the power and control of Satan. But that's not the way things are. Here's the way the world works:

> The LORD does whatever pleases him throughout all heaven and earth, and on the seas and in their depths. He causes the clouds to rise over the earth. He sends the lightning with the rain and releases the wind from his storehouses. (Psalm 135:6–7)

We are so quick to give God credit for the beautiful sunrise or the drought-breaking rain or the magnificent mountains. But when it comes to fires, hurricanes, and earthquakes, we want to keep God out of it (even though we often call them "acts of God"). We can't bear to think that the same God who causes a flower to bloom also causes a tornado to rip through a trailer park.

We know, we know, you're fighting this notion right about now, and we don't blame you. This isn't easy to accept, which is why we're not asking you to accept it just yet. We've taken time to think about it and to consider what the Bible has to say, along with the works of some very wise people who have wrestled with this difficult subject a lot longer than we have. We're going to dig into the next Minor Prophet in our study and see what he has to say. But before we do that, we want to give you something else to think about.

All Is Not Right with the World

The way the world is now is not the way God intended it to be. In the beginning, God created a perfect world. When He came to the end of the creation process, the Bible says: "Then God looked over all he had made, and he saw that it was excellent in every way" (Genesis 1:31).

There was no suffering, no pain, no disease, no earthquakes, no floods, no famine, and no destruction. It was truly heaven on earth. Then sin—that's anything that falls short of God's perfect standard—entered the world when God's created beings decided to disobey Him. God placed a curse on Adam and Eve, and ever since then the sin virus has infected every human being (Romans 3:23).

Not only that, but the sin virus has infected the earth as well. Because of Adam's sin and the sin of his wife, God said He would place "a curse on the ground." Instead of producing only good and beautiful things, God told Adam that the earth "will grow thorns and thistles for you, though you will eat of its grains" (Genesis 3:17, 18).

Sin isn't a terribly popular word these days, because sin is very personal. There's that awful guilt thing, and who wants to deal with that? So in order to take the attention off ourselves, we've developed alternate ways of describing our offenses:

- Mistakes were made
- An unfortunate error occurred
- I was misunderstood

But the fact is, we all sin. Every one of us. We know it, you know it, and most of all, God knows it. And you know what else? It ticks Him off. It ticked Him off when Adam and Eve sinned the first time, and it ticks Him off now. Besides offending God personally, sin has messed up this beautiful universe He made. It doesn't work the way God designed it. It wasn't supposed to decay and it wasn't supposed to destroy, but that's the way things are because of the curse of sin:

> Against its will, everything on earth was subjected to God's curse. . . . For we know that all creation has been groaning as in the pains of childbirth right up to the present time. (Romans 8:20, 22)

So we have earthquakes and hurricanes and floods and famine. And we worry about the depletion of the ozone layer and global warming and rogue comets—all because we live in a sinful world. And if that's not enough to think about when you put your factor-97 sunscreen on before going outside, consider this little fact:

GOD USES NATURE TO GET OUR ATTENTION

Just as God uses the stunning beauty of His created world to bring glory to Himself (read Psalm 19), He also uses the unfriendly forces of nature to wake us up to the reality of sin in the world and in our lives. He's definitely ticked off at what's going on because of sin, and He wants us to know why.

Before you get mad at God for being mad at you, you need to know that God is not capricious or spiteful in anything He does. His acts are not senseless and unreasonable. Even though we cannot possibly understand everything God does (Isaiah 55:8), we can be confident that everything He does is fair and just. And if He uses a natural disaster to get our attention, He is only doing it for our own good. That's the message of Joel, the next Minor Prophet we'll talk about.

Joel and the Grasshoppers

The book of Joel opens dramatically. The year is 825 B.C. (give or take a few years) and a natural disaster of biblical proportions has hit the southern kingdom of Judah. This wasn't your everyday run-of-the-mill disaster like we see on CNN. This was a plague of locusts.

Now before you brush this off as a mild problem (kind of like the alleged killer-bee invasion we were warned about several years ago), you need to know that this was serious. "In all your history, has anything like this ever happened before?" Joel asks (1:2). Evidently not, because Joel encourages the people to "Pass the awful story down from generation to generation" (1:3).

The Minor Prophet Makes a Major Stink

When tragedy strikes, it's often our tendency to downplay it, or at least to focus on our resolve to overcome rather than to emphasize

Locust Facts

Locusts are actually migratory grasshoppers capable of inflicting great harm to crops wherever they swarm. Have you ever heard of something called a "scorched earth policy"? It's a military term describing what happens when one side in a battle blows up, destroys, and literally burns anything that would be of use to the enemy. That's what locust swarms are capable of doing, and this is what the locusts did to Judah. They decimated every square inch of vegetation, leaving the earth looking as though it had been burned.

the tragedy itself. We want our leaders and experts to tell us that everything is going to be fine. Even when we experience personal difficulties, we don't want to hear that we're really bad off. We could be sitting in the emergency room with a gaping head wound, and we hope some doctor will say, "Oh, you'll be up and around in no time."

Joel has no intention of being so comforting. Far from downplaying the locust disaster, Joel tells the people that this is the worst possible thing that could have happened to them. And just to make sure that everyone realizes the serious nature of this unprecedented invasion, Joel targets three socioeconomic groups:

- To the *leaders* he says, "Never forget this terrible event" (1:3).
- He makes sure the *drunks* realize that their source of booze (fermented grapes) has been wiped out (1:5).
- Joel tells the *farmers* that they won't be bringing any fruit to market for a few years (1:11).

It may seem like overkill for this prophet of God to get in everyone's faces about the locusts. You would think that the scorched earth would be enough to convince the people of Judah that they had a problem on their hands, but evidently they were treating the disaster rather lightly. So Joel had to get their attention.

It's always been this way with humans and natural disasters. At first we're shocked and maybe even bothered, but then we get back to business as usual. We do our best to put the disaster out of our minds.

"Montana is on fire? Hey, it happens every summer."

"A mud slide has killed thousands in Iran? Aren't they our enemy?"

"Millions are dying of starvation in India? (Yawn) Let's go to Starbucks."

And so it goes. We hear about something tragic, we process it for a moment, then we shrug our shoulders indifferently. There's only one problem. Such indifference really ticks God off. Do you really think that God allows—and sometimes causes—such devastation to occur merely to provide a story line for CNN? Are we to treat these world disasters like some big-budget Hollywood movie? God forbid that we do. And He does.

The Day of the Lord

Joel compares the locusts to an advancing army and describes their invasion in horrifying detail. Then he makes it clear as to who is responsible for this devastating event:

> The LORD leads them with a shout! This is his mighty army, and they follow his orders. The day of the LORD is an awesome, terrible thing. Who can endure it? (2:11).

The phrase *day of the Lord* is repeated five times in the book of Joel (and bunches of other times in some of the other Minor Prophets). Theologians agree that this always refers to some extraordinary event that has either just happened (like the locust plague) or will happen in the future. "Day of the Lord" also indicates the final period in human history when God will once and for all defeat the forces of evil and reward the faithful.

> The day of the LORD is on the way, the day when destruction comes from the Almighty. How terrible that day will be! (1:15)

A lot of people can't believe God could be so cruel. Unable to come to a reasonable conclusion, they take the easy way out. They turn their backs on God because they can't possibly believe in a God who would bring about such destruction—now or in the future.

What they don't realize is that humanity has already turned its back on God. We're running away from Him. But rather than let us run to our own eternal destruction, God is doing things to get our attention so that we will turn back around and see Him for who He really is: the God of love who wants to save us.

This isn't easy to deal with. We have so underestimated God, and we so overestimate ourselves, that we have trouble coming to grips with a God of love who allows people to die because of the disasters He causes. But come to grips with it we must.

Perhaps a little illustration will help. Imagine for a minute that you are a parent (this may not take any imagination for you at all). You love your child. You don't want him hurt. So you tell him, "Don't ride your bike in the street." But your kid disobeys your directive and takes his bike into traffic. You see it happen and you are terrified and angry. You scold your child and then impose a punishment by taking away the bike for a week. Why? Are you being mean? Do you enjoy the discipline process? No, it's tough, but you do it anyway because you don't want something worse to happen.

That's the picture here. God loves us so much that He has given us some warnings. They may be very personal, or something on a much larger scale. Whatever God uses to get our attention (or the attention of humanity in general), He uses it because He doesn't want something far worse to happen to us. We have to realize that the things He uses are on a bigger scale because the consequences of refusing to reverse our courses are final and eternal.

What It Means to Turn Back to God

The whole point of Joel's book of prophecy is to convince people to turn away from their path of sin, which leads to destruction, and to turn toward God, the source of eternal life. That is the essence of repentance. When you hear the word *repentance,* perhaps you have this image of falling to your knees before God, begging for forgiveness. While that reaction can happen, repentance is much more logical than that. Here's what Eugene Peterson writes:

> Repentance is not an emotion. It is not feeling sorry for your sins. It is a decision. It is deciding that you have been wrong in supposing that you could manage your own life and be your own god; it is deciding that you were wrong in thinking that you had, or could get, the strength, education and training to make it on your own; it is deciding that you have been told a pack of lies about yourself and your neighbors and your world. And it is deciding that God in Jesus Christ is telling you the truth.[1]

There is a definite correlation between the disasters God causes and repentance. "God's arrows are judgments aimed at provoking repentance," Peterson concludes. This is exactly why God told people of Judah in Joel's day, "Turn to me now, while there is time! Give me your hearts" (2:12). He wanted them to avoid the much bigger disaster that would make the locust plague look like a walk in the park. And just in case you think this is a message only for people in the Old Testament, here's what the New Testament has to say:

> For God can use sorrow in our lives to help us turn away from sin and seek salvation. We will never regret that kind of sorrow. But sorrow without repentance is the kind that results in death. (2 Corinthians 7:10)

No doubt Pain as God's megaphone is a terrible instrument; it may lead to final and unrepented rebellion. But it gives the only opportunity the bad man can have for amendment. It removes the veil; it plants the flag of truth within the fortress of the rebel soul.

—C. S. Lewis

What God Wants

Sin has ticked God off. It's messed up His world. It has changed who we are in relation to God. But sin hasn't changed who God is. "I am the LORD, and I do not change," God says to His people through the prophet Malachi (Malachi 3:6).

We so badly want to please God with our little acts of goodness and self-sacrifice. We think that by going to church a few times a year, by dropping a few dollars in the collection plate, and by trying to live a "good" life, we will get on God's good side. As long as the scales of divine justice tip a little more to the good than the bad, God will love us enough to save us.

But that's not how it works. There's nothing we can do to earn God's favor (Ephesians 2:8–9). There is nothing about us that's good enough for God (remember that sin thing), and God is fully aware of our shortcomings. That's why He doesn't want our effort; He wants our hearts. King David wrote in the Psalms:

> You would not be pleased with sacrifices, or I would bring them. If I brought you a burnt offering, you would not accept it. The sacrifice you want is a broken spirit. A broken and repentant heart, O God, you will not despise. (51:16–17)

That's exactly what God says here in the book of Joel: "Don't tear your clothing in your grief; instead, tear your hearts" (2:13).

Not Just for Unbelievers

Turning back to God isn't just for those who don't have a personal relationship with God. Repentance is for Christians as well. Just because God has forgiven your sins once and for all, you can still tick God off with your sin. God still needs for you to turn back *to* Him after you've turned your back *on* Him.

A lot of people think that God uses natural disasters just to get the attention of unbelievers. No, God uses natural disasters to get the attention of *sinners,* and that includes all of us. In fact, you could make a case that God's people are the first ones who need to repent and come back to God whenever natural disasters occur. Christians love to quote 2 Chronicles 7:14, but they rarely include the verse immediately preceding it. Not only do these verses apply to the prophet Joel and the things he was dealing with, but they also relate directly to us in the twenty-first century:

> At times I might shut up the heavens so that no rain falls, or I might command locusts to devour your crops, or I might send plagues among you. Then if my people who are called by my name will humble themselves and pray and seek my face and turn from their wicked ways, I will hear from heaven and will forgive their sins and heal their land. (2 Chronicles 7:13–14)

Regardless of who you are or what you've done, God wants you back. Are you staying away from God because you are afraid of what He might do to you? Do you think your sins are so bad that He can't forgive you? You need to know that the God who causes disasters is also the God who loves you completely. There's nothing good you could do to make God love you any more, and there's nothing bad you could do to make God love you any less.

Love defines the very essence of God. He hates sin, but he loves you. Yes, you tick him off, but he wants you back. James Montgomery Boice writes:

> Are you one whose life has been destroyed by the locusts of sin? Has sin stripped your life of every green thing, so that it seems a spiritual desert? If so, you need to return to the One who alone can make life grow fruitful again. Only God can restore the years that have been eaten away.[2]

What God Offers

The one true God of the Bible offers nothing but love, forgiveness, and acceptance to all who will come back to Him.

> Return to the LORD your God, for he is gracious and merciful. He is not easily angered. He is filled with kindness and is eager not to punish you. (Joel 2:13)

Joel lists five qualities of God's amazing personality, all of which He displays to all who repent:

God is gracious. By definition, grace is God giving us what we don't deserve. It is God's special favor. We deserve to die in our sins, but God offers eternal life instead. The essence of grace is found in the most famous verse in the Bible:

> For God so loved the world that he gave his only Son, so that everyone who believes in him will not perish but have eternal life. (John 3:16)

God is merciful. Mercy is closely related to grace (and you'll often find it in the same context), but the meaning is slightly different. God's mercy means that He isn't giving us what we deserve. God has every right to destroy us, but He doesn't. Nehemiah praises God for taking Israel back after they repented from their rebellion:

> But in your great mercy, you did not destroy them completely or abandon them forever. What a gracious and merciful God you are! (Nehemiah 9:31)

God is not easily angered. Yes, God gets angry. He gets ticked off. But not easily and not without great provocation. We should not take God's anger lightly, but neither should we let it keep us from turning back to Him. Read what God says about Himself:

> I am the LORD, the merciful and gracious God. I am slow to anger and rich in unfailing love and faithfulness. (Exodus 34:6)

God is filled with kindness. Kindness is love in action. It means that you don't merely tell people you love them; you show them. God has expressed His kindness toward us in the most extravagant manner possible. We deserve to die, but He sent Jesus to die in our place:

> So we praise God for the wonderful kindness he has poured out on us. . . . He is so rich in kindness that he purchased our

freedom through the blood of his Son, and our sins are forgiven. He has showered his kindness on us, along with all
wisdom and understanding. (Ephesians 1:6, 8)

God is eager not to punish you. God doesn't enjoy punishing people
but neither is He sitting back while the world goes down the tubes. In
that final "day of the Lord," God's judgment and justice will come, but
He is deliberately holding back so that more people will turn to Him:

> The Lord isn't really being slow about his promise to return,
> as some people think. No, he is being patient for your sake.
> He does not want anyone to perish, so he is giving more time
> for everyone to repent. (2 Peter 3:9)

And Now for the Really Good News

Remember when you were a kid and you did something you knew
your parents wouldn't like? Your first instinct was to cover up the
deed by running off. But then your conscience started to gnaw at you
and you decided to face the consequences rather then endure the
pangs of guilt. So you told your dad or your mom (hoping she would
butter up your dad) and then you waited for the punishment. Only
your parents didn't punish you. Instead, they hugged you and threw a
big party!

OK, so maybe that never happened, but that's exactly what happens
when someone turns back to God. Jesus said, "In the same way, there
is joy in the presence of God's angels when even one sinner repents"
(Luke 15:10). Then he told the story of the prodigal son, who came
back home to his father after a period of rebellion. Rather than discipline him, the father embraced his son and then threw a party. "He was
lost, but now he is found!" the father said (Luke 15:32).

Joel says the same thing to the people of Judah (only he's not quite
sure):

> Who knows? Perhaps even yet he will give you a reprieve,
> sending you a blessing instead of this terrible curse. Perhaps

he will give you so much that you will be able to offer grain
and wine to the LORD your God as before! (2:14)

Then he quotes God, who confirms Joel's statement:

I will give you back what you lost to the stripping locusts, the
cutting locusts, the swarming locusts, and the hopping locusts.
It was I who sent this great destroying army against you. Once
again you will have all the food you want, and you will praise
the LORD your God, who does these miracles for you. (2:25–26)

Don't take this to mean that God is going to make you rich. What
it means is that God "will supply all your needs from his glorious
riches, which have been given to us in Christ Jesus" (Philippians
4:19). More important, when you come back to God in genuine repentance, God will restore to you the joy of His salvation (Psalm
51:12). It's like experiencing your first love all over again. Only it's
God who does all the loving, like He always has. Your repentance
simply opens your eyes and your heart to the reality of God's love.

A Few Lessons Before We Move On

We need to thank God that He is in control of nature. We need to be
thankful that natural disasters, as bad as they can be, are not the
norm. We enjoy more beautiful days than bad. The sea, the snow, and
even the rain provide endless pleasure. God designed the weather
cycles and temperatures more for sustaining us than destroying us.
Besides, as Erwin Lutzer observes, "If nature is out of God's hands,
then my life is also out of His hands."[3]

We can't take natural disasters lightly. We've already touched on
this, but we need to bring it up again. When natural disasters strike,
we should never brush them off or say that certain people deserve
them. This is completely wrong, and God won't tolerate it. Christians
should be the first to give aid to those who are in distress. We need
to pray for those who are hurting and help wherever we can.

In addition, we need to understand that natural disasters, no matter where they happen, are a sign that God's judgment is coming for all people. When a man-made tower killed eighteen men, Jesus said, "Were they the worst sinners in Jerusalem? No, and I tell you again that unless you repent, you will also perish" (Luke 13:4–5). Death is no respecter of persons.

The only way to escape judgment is by turning back to God. There's the once-for-all repentance that leads to salvation—the kind Peter was talking about when he preached: "Now turn from your sins and turn to God, so you can be cleansed of your sins" (Acts 3:19). And then there's the practical, repeatable repentance in which you recognize and confess your sin when it pops up. This is the kind that puts you back in touch with God after your sin has kept you from Him (1 John 1:9). Either way, it's the only way to get right with God, and therefore the only way to experience the hope He offers.

It may seem strange to end this chapter on a positive note. After all, we've covered natural disasters, death, and judgment. Not exactly topics that inspire hope and confidence. But there's no other way to end it, not because we are eternal optimists, but because God has an eternal plan.

Yes, the earth is under the curse of sin, the same curse that plagues us and gives us so much trouble. There are natural disasters of all kinds, causing immense human pain and suffering. But the Creator of all things, the God who loves us and who is in complete control, is not deterred by the way things are. He has big plans in place, and those plans include all creation and everyone who has turned back to God.

> All creation anticipates the day when it will join God's children in glorious freedom from death and decay. For we know that all creation has been groaning as in the pains of childbirth right up to the present time. And even we Christians, although we have the Holy Spirit within us as a foretaste of future glory, also groan to be released from pain and suffering. We, too, wait anxiously for that day when God will give us our full rights as his children, including the new bodies he has promised us. Now that we are saved, we eagerly look forward to this freedom. (Romans 8:21–24)

3

THE GREEDY AND THE NEEDY

In response to rising statistics of juvenile crime, society has implemented a "feel good about yourself" campaign. Of course, that slogan doesn't sound very sophisticated, so a bunch of politicians, educators, welfare workers, and psychologists came up with "self-esteem enhancement." The idea is simply this: If we make kids feel better about themselves, then they won't get into so much trouble.

While we don't know if these efforts will have a positive impact on our society, we aren't sure that the problem has been accurately analyzed. In our humble (but correct) opinion, the feelings of many children and adults about themselves are already overinflated.

Most of us don't suffer from low self-esteem; on the contrary, our problem is an exaggerated sense of self-importance. Maybe that is why some people *do* have a low self-image. The rest of us think so highly of ourselves that we make others feel as if they could never rise to our level. They feel inferior because we act superior.

When a hyperactive ego is combined with economic prosperity, you have the perfect formula for arrogance. People with that combination believe that they deserve their wealth. They are entitled to have what others don't because those other folks are "second-class." Attitudes of pride and arrogance cause us to disregard the value of others who haven't achieved our social or financial statuses. We don't care about *them* because . . . well, because it's all about us. We might as well have a license plate frame that reads, "All for one, and I'm the one."

Wait a minute. Maybe it's not entirely true that our arrogance makes us disparage *everyone* else. There are some people we appreciate—

those who are in our social class—but the poor and the disadvantaged are another story. Their contributions to society are often considered negligible. The prevailing view is that there is no reason to care about them; our contribution to the welfare system is enough. As Ebenezer Scrooge said,

> Let the poor and the destitute go to the work camps or the poor house. My taxes help to support those public institutions, and they cost enough. Those who are badly off must go there. If they would rather die than to go to those places, then maybe they ought to do so and decrease the world's population.[1]

Why are we making such a big deal about people's arrogance and their indifference toward the poor? Because it is a very big deal to God. It is such a big deal that:

God Is Ticked off When We Oppress or Neglect the Poor

None of us is inclined to think that we treat the poor with disrespect, and we certainly don't abuse or oppress them. There are times when we actually help them out with charitable contributions to a relief organization or a handout to a homeless person. We might even help serve up Thanksgiving Day dinner at the rescue mission. So, how can we be criticized for ignoring the poor? At our worst, we are just indifferent to them. Is that such a terrible sin?

Before you try to soothe your conscience or justify your actions and attitudes, perhaps we ought to review the message that Amos brought to the Israelites about this very issue.

Not-So-Famous Amos

Although their messages weren't usually popular with the people, the prophets were recognized as God's authorized representatives. Most of them went through an official instruction process. Samuel, the first prophet after Moses, actually started a training program for fledgling prophets. It was a type of vocational school where the laws of Moses were used as curriculum. It even had several campuses.

There was one prophet, however, who never enrolled in a single class at the prophets' alma mater. Amos was a farmer, and he didn't start out to be a prophet. But later in life, God gave him a message and told him to proclaim it to the northern kingdom of Israel.

> I'm not one of your professional prophets. I certainly never trained to be one. I'm just a shepherd, and I take care of fig trees. But the LORD called me away from my flock and told me, "Go and prophesy to my people in Israel." (Amos 7:14–15)

The name *Amos* means "burden bearer" in Hebrew, an appropriate name because it was a particularly difficult burden for him to preach God's message. He started with three strikes against him:

Strike 1: He lacked the usual credentials of a prophet because he could not list a degree from Prophets' University on his resume.

Strike 2: He was an outsider. Tekoa was in the southern kingdom of Judah, but God told him to preach to the residents of Israel. Crossing tribal boundaries to pronounce judgment didn't do much for his popularity.

Strike 3: He brought a critical message. This was nothing new for the Minor Prophets; they all brought unpleasant messages. But Amos was less tactful than the other prophets (who had probably had a class in diplomacy). He told the priest of Bethel that his wife would become a prostitute and referred to the rich women of Israel as "fat cows." Winning friends was not his strong suit.

Amos arrived in Israel sometime around 755 B.C. Prosperity in the region was at an all-time high. Threats from other enemy nations were at an all-time low. The people in Israel were enjoying unprecedented peace and affluence. Well, not all of the people; just the rich ones. The poor people of Israel were suffering under the oppression of the ruling class.

Pity the Fool Who Oppresses the Poor

God didn't object to the affluence enjoyed by the residents of Israel. After all, God's blessings often include material wealth. But in their prosperity, the people of Israel had become greedy, selfish, and unjust. Illegal and immoral slavery was the result of their overtaxation of the poor and their land-grabbing schemes against the disadvantaged.

Amos didn't pull any punches when he relayed God's displeasure with Israel for its cruelty and indifference toward the poor.

> This is what the LORD says: "The people of Israel have sinned again and again, and I will not forget it. I will not let them go unpunished any longer! They have perverted justice by selling honest people for silver and poor people for a pair of sandals. They trample helpless people in the dust and deny justice to those who are oppressed. (2:6–7)

He blatantly confronted the ways in which the legal system was manipulated against the poor, subjecting them to economic exploitation.

> You wicked people! You twist justice, making it a bitter pill for the poor and oppressed. Righteousness and fair play are meaningless fictions to you. . . . You trample the poor and steal what little they have through taxes and unfair rent. . . . You oppress good people by taking bribes and deprive the poor of justice in the courts. (5:7, 11–12)

The rich of Israel hid behind a facade of religion, but in their hearts they ruthlessly cheated the poor and unfortunate who were helpless to protect themselves.

> Listen to this, you who rob the poor and trample the needy! You can't wait for the Sabbath day to be over and the religious festivals to end so you can get back to cheating the helpless. You measure out your grain in false measures and weigh it out on dishonest scales. And you mix the wheat you sell with chaff swept from the floor! Then you enslave poor people for a debt of one piece of silver or a pair of sandals. (8:4–6)

Could This Be a Case of Prejudice Against the Prosperous?

Could it be that Amos was biased in favor of the poor just because he was one of them? Could his vehemence against the wealthy have been fueled by his jealousy of their wealth? Hardly. Amos was unduly modest when he said: "I'm just a shepherd, and I take care of fig trees." Don't think that he was some lethargic rent-a-watchman for someone's wool supply, or that he had two potted fruit trees in his apartment above the wool-shearing shack.

The usual Hebrew word for shepherd is *roeh,* but the word used by Amos to describe himself was *noqed,* which seems to indicate a "sheep breeder" instead of just a guy who watches the flock. Bible scholars believe he managed or owned large herds of sheep and goats and was in charge of other shepherds. In addition, he was a rancher with orchards of Sycamore figs. Every indication is that Amos was a successful businessman. He was a landowner who engaged in separate businesses of livestock breeding, ranching, and farming.

Here Comes the Judgment

God was ticked off and fed up with the greediness of Israel, and He was not going to tolerate its injustice any longer. Amos proclaimed that God's judgment was just around the corner in the form of an attack, invasion, and capture by an enemy nation.

Consider the irony of the message that Amos preached. Because they had enslaved and oppressed the poor (among other offenses), an enemy would soon conquer Israel, and the rich of Israel would themselves become slaves.

This was not a case in which God woke up on the wrong side of a cloud one morning and decided to take it out on Israel. In the preceding decades and centuries, God had given warnings to the people of Israel in an attempt to get their attention and persuade them to turn back to Him. But they apparently ignored these previous warnings as just "natural" disasters. So, they refused to see God as the cause of:

- **Famines:** "I brought hunger to every city and famine to every town. But still you wouldn't return to me," says the LORD. (4:6)
- **Droughts:** "I kept the rain from falling when you needed it the most, ruining all your crops. . . . But still you wouldn't return to me," says the LORD. (4:7–8)
- **Crop failures:** "I struck your farms and vineyards with blight and mildew. Locusts devoured all your fig and olive trees. But still you wouldn't return to me," says the LORD. (4:9)
- **Death from plagues and war:** "I sent plagues against you like the plagues I sent against Egypt long ago. . . . The stench of death filled the air! But still you wouldn't return to me," says the LORD. (4:10)
- **Urban disasters:** I destroyed some of your cities, as I destroyed Sodom and Gomorrah. Those of you who survived were like half-burned sticks snatched from a fire. But still you wouldn't return to me," says the LORD. (4:11)

The people of Israel had proved themselves oblivious to God's discipline in the past. Amos wanted to be sure that they got the point this time. In language that was both plain and powerful, Amos declared that the calamity to come was the result of God's judgment and not just a fluke of nature or bad luck:

"O people of Israel, I am about to bring an enemy nation against you," says the LORD God Almighty. "It will oppress you bitterly throughout your land." (6:14)

And with a dramatic flair that must have inspired those "Prepare to meet your maker" lines in action movies, Amos proclaimed:

Prepare to meet your God as he comes in judgment, you people of Israel! (4:12)

Wow! Hearing that last sentence would be enough to ruin your day and make you clean up your act—or so you would think. But it had no impact whatsoever on the nation of Israel. It continued in its unrighteous ways. So, about thirty years later (in 722 B.C.), just as Amos had prophesied, the Assyrian army captured Israel.

Does Amos Shame Us?

Every one of the Minor Prophets communicated the theme of God's holiness and His forgiveness. Within that context, each prophet identified how the people had fallen short of God's standard and angered Him with their outrageous behavior. God often responded with judgment as part of the punishment they deserved for their wrongful acts and attitudes, and as discipline to turn them back to Himself.

Although the messages of the Minor Prophets are almost three thousand years old, they are relevant to our culture. Hopefully, as Christians in the twenty-first century, we can heed the warnings that Amos was unable to impress upon Israel.

Warning #1: We tick God off with our lack of social conscience because it reflects an insincere faith.

There is no denying it. Amos said it clearly and succinctly. God is offended when we don't attend to the poor and those less fortunate than ourselves. He wants us to have a social conscience that makes us sensitive to the needs of others, particularly the poor.

Maybe the people of Israel didn't believe this aspect of Amos's message. Maybe they thought God wouldn't really get that worked up over their dishonest dealings with the poor. Maybe they didn't believe that their behavior really warranted an outpouring of God's wrath. Couldn't the problem be rectified with just a little sensitivity training?

Let's not make the mistake of thinking that God overreacted. His response was not out of proportion—He saw the bigger picture. The people's treatment of the poor was just a symptom of a larger problem. They were religious (with all of their festivals and rituals), but they weren't spiritual.

Amos hammered on Israel for its spiritual hypocrisy. They pretended that they loved God, but their oppression of the poor proved that they had hard hearts, unresponsive to God. God considered their religious attitudes to be completely phony:

> I hate all your show and pretense—the hypocrisy of your religious festivals and solemn assemblies. I will not accept your burnt offerings and grain offerings. I won't even notice

all your choice peace offerings. Away with your hymns of praise! They are only noise to my ears. (5:21–23)

To put it bluntly, God knew that the people of Israel didn't love Him because they didn't show love to others. This is a fundamental principle of the Christian faith. A sincere love for God produces a love for other people.

Scripture is replete with verses that equate a love for God with a love for other people. If you don't have the former, then you don't have the latter. Here is how Jesus said it:

> God is love, and all who live in love live in God, and God lives in them. . . . We love each other as a result of his loving us first. If someone says, "I love God," but hates a Christian brother or sister, that person is a liar; for if we don't love people we can see, how can we love God, whom we have not seen? (1 John 4:16, 19–20)

If God's love is in us, then we should be willing to use our resources to help those who are in need:

> But if anyone has enough money to live well and sees a brother or sister in need and refuses to help—how can God's love be in that person? (1 John 3:17)

It isn't enough that we have love for other Christians. God's love should make us sensitive to everyone who suffers:

> Pure and lasting religion in the sight of God our Father means that we must care for orphans and widows in their troubles, and refuse to let the world corrupt us. (James 1:27)

Let's stop shaking our fingers at the people of Israel and examine ourselves. How about us? Are we guilty of the same type of spiritual hypocrisy? Shouldn't we find out? Do you want to test whether you really love God? OK, then, it's gut-check time:

- Do you view the homeless with contempt or compassion?
- Is your attention, concern, or affection for people influenced by factors of race, ethnicity, citizenship, or net worth?
- Do you ignore the needs of the poor?
- Are you more interested in satisfying your own greed than in helping someone else obtain the necessities of life?
- Do you just feel bad for the poor and the oppressed, or do you act compassionately to stop injustice for the disadvantaged?
- Is giving money to the homeless shelters in your own community a burden or a blessing?

Answer these questions honestly and then respond accordingly. Don't make the colossal blunder of the Israelites who didn't think that God was serious about this.

> Poverty is not wholly a personal failure. . . . Poverty is a reflection also on those who are not poor.
>
> —Bruce Atkinson

Warning #2: If we don't snap out of it, God may need to bring hardship upon us to get our attention.

Not all problems, difficulties, and hardships that befall us are punishments from God. We live in a world where evil exists, and sometimes we suffer the effects of that evil without it being imposed by God. Though it happens within the context of His sovereignty, He does not instigate it. But we are naive, perhaps like the Israelites, if we think that God represses His anger but does not act. Amos mocked those who exposed their ignorance of God by saying, "Nothing bad will happen to us." (9:10)

The message of Amos was clear: God intentionally inflicted adversity upon Israel in the past (famine, drought, disease, and war) as a warning to bring the people back to Him (Amos 4:6–10). But because of Israel's failure to heed His warnings, God was going to intentionally bring about the country's demise:

I am determined to bring disaster upon them and not to help them. (Amos 9:4)

God is not inept or infirm. He is not apathetic or absent-minded. If we tick Him off, He is capable of and willing to bring discipline into our lives to straighten us out. He loves us that much.

Warning #3: We aren't exempt from God's discipline just because He has blessed us in the past. He expects more from us if we claim Him as our heavenly Father.

The Israelites in the northern kingdom were the descendants of Abraham. They were part of God's chosen people. And yet, God brought judgment upon them. God does not show favoritism (Romans 2:11). Israel was not exempt from God's judgment simply because she held special status with God. Similarly, we can't think that we are exempt from God's judgment simply because our nation has experienced His favor and blessings in the past.

Because Israel was familiar with God's precepts and had a covenant relationship with Him, God rightly expected more obedience from Israel than from the pagan nations. In fact, Amos indicates that Israel had a higher obligation for holiness *because* she was part of God's family:

> Listen to this message that the LORD has spoken against you, O people of Israel and Judah—the entire family I rescued from Egypt: "From among all the families on the earth, I chose you alone. That is why I must punish you for all your sins." (3:1–2)

But Israel does not have exclusive rights to a privileged position with God. We can claim to be part of His family as well:

> Therefore, since we have been made right in God's sight by faith, we have peace with God because of what Jesus Christ our Lord has done for us. Because of our faith, Christ has brought us into this place of highest privilege where we now stand. (Romans 5:1–2)

As part of His family, "we know how dearly God loves us, because he has given us the Holy Spirit to fill our hearts with his love" (Romans 5:5). Since we have the knowledge of God and His love, He holds us accountable for our obligation to extend that love to others.

The Amos Solution to the Socioeconomic Problem

Amos spelled it out very plainly: God is upset by social injustice. It should not be permitted or tolerated. And when it exists, the situation should be remedied.

God's plea, spoken through Amos, has a familiar ring to it. Perhaps you have heard it before, as it has echoed repeatedly in legislative sessions across our country. Of course, special-interest groups, lobbyists, and politicians never give credit to Amos for the idea. That's understandable. The important point is that the message is brought into public discourse. We need to recognize the fact that social injustice exists and that it needs to be corrected.

Many people can identify problems and complain about what needs to be changed. That's the easy part. The more difficult task is to devise a solution to the problem. When it comes to solving the issues of socioeconomic disparities in our culture, there has been a lot of complaining but little solving. Despite the attempts of all of the social welfare organizations and elected officials over the past decades, little progress has been made.

But fret not. Amos is the man. Not only did he draw attention to the problems of social injustice, he also presented the solution.

Surprisingly, the solution proposed by Amos had nothing to do with the redistribution of wealth. Rather than throwing money at the problem, Amos recommended that the primary solution be a *spiritual* response, not a *financial* one.

In his tirade, Amos condemned Israel for its lack of social conscience, and he told the nation the precise way to correct the malady:

> Now this is what the LORD says to the family of Israel: "Come back to me and live!" (5:4)

And just in case they didn't pick up on it, he reiterated the solution:

> Come back to the LORD and live! If you don't, he will roar
> through Israel like a fire, devouring you completely. (5:6)

Tax dollars, tutoring, welfare relief, counseling, vocational training, employment incentives, and other forms of social action might
help, but these worthwhile activities won't change attitudes. The real
solution involves a change of heart.

Instead of pursuing a political ideology to solve the problem, we
need to pursue God. We need to reconnect with Him. If we change
only our external behavior, we will be guilty of the same type of spiritual hypocrisy for which Amos chastised Israel. God isn't impressed
with forced and contrived conduct or with manipulated methodol-
ogy. He desires us to be *receptive* to His love, so that we will *reflect*
His love to others.

> I hate all your show and pretense—the hypocrisy of your reli-
> gious festivals and solemn assemblies. . . . Instead, I want to
> see a mighty flood of justice, a river of righteous living that
> will never run dry. (5:21, 24)

Which brings us to the message of hope embedded in the procla-
mation of Amos. As with every other Minor Prophet, Amos empha-
sizes that God allows us the opportunity to return to Him in love. As
offensive as He may find our conduct, the severity of our sin never
outweighs the strength of His love. He is anxious to restore a close,
intimate relationship with us, and He promises to do so if we return
to Him:

> Do what is good and run from evil—that you may live! Then
> the LORD God Almighty will truly be your helper, just as you
> have claimed he is. Hate evil and love what is good; remodel
> your courts into true halls of justice. Perhaps even yet the
> LORD God Almighty will have mercy on his people who
> remain. (5:14–15)

4

PRIDE GOES BEFORE THE FALL . . .
AND EVERYTHING ELSE

Jim is normally a mild-mannered guy, but a few years ago something happened in a grocery-store line that ticked him off. There he was minding his own business, waiting to pay for some milk and eggs, when the guy standing in line in front of Jim casually turned around and said, "How about them Dogs? Are they the greatest or what?"

Now there are a few things you need to know before we continue our story. The "Dogs" the guy was referring to are the Bulldogs, or more specifically, the Fresno State Bulldogs. Like a lot of locals, we happen to think Fresno State is a fine university, a great place to get a degree in agriculture, criminology, or oenology, the science of making wine (those three majors speak volumes about Fresno). But despite its growing reputation and formidable local support, Fresno State will probably never achieve the status enjoyed by California's big-time universities, such as Stanford and USC.

One area in which Fresno State has come close to the big time is sports, specifically football. The Fresno State football team has the reputation of being willing to play "anybody anytime," and sometimes they succeed at showing up a major university on its home turf. Such was the case when Fresno State beat USC in the 1993 Freedom Bowl. Nobody expected it, but when the Bulldogs whipped the USC Trojans, a perennial powerhouse, the city went delirious.

There's one other tidbit of information that adds color to our story about Jim and the guy in the grocery-store line. The man who made the comment about the "Dogs" was wearing a red Bulldog cap and a red Bulldog sweatshirt that was stretched to its limit around his considerable girth. Jim, who is six-foot-four and built like a Navy Seal, was wearing a shirt from his alma mater—USC.

Jim kindly agreed that it was quite an achievement, the Bulldogs beating USC and all. But Mr. Bulldog couldn't leave it alone. "Guess you USC guys aren't so good after all," he said. Jim is a patient man, and he was quite willing to let the buffoon in front of him in the grocery-store line revel in his glory, but he had gone too far. Mr. Bulldog unleashed another torrent of superlatives about how great Fresno State was and how pathetic USC was, ending it by saying, "So, are you wearing USC underwear under that sweatshirt?"

Very calmly, very quietly, Jim took one step forward and said to the man, "No, actually, I'm wearing a Beretta 9mm pistol, and you're really beginning to tick me off."

Needless to say, Mr. Bulldog turned ashen, and the grocery clerk stopped in midscan. Somehow she managed to finish the transaction, and the man left quickly without saying another word. As for Jim—who just happens to be the chief criminologist for the Fresno County Sheriff's department—he paid for his milk and eggs and left, but not before telling the clerk to have a nice day.

Though Jim would be the last person to compare himself to God, we would like to make a comparison between Jim's reaction to the nagging weasel in the grocery-store line and God's reaction to us when we insist on telling God how great we are:

GOD IS TICKED OFF BY OUR PRIDE

Does this surprise you? Isn't pride a good thing? Well, yes and no. There's good pride and then there's the pride that ticks God off. God isn't bothered by the kind of pride that you feel when someone you care about—a child, an employee, a spouse, or a brother—does something really well. And the kind of pride you take in achieving something very important, like a good grade or a job promotion, doesn't even raise an eyebrow. No, the kind of pride that ticks God off is the same kind that ticked Jim off. This is unabashed, in-your-face pride that's rooted in arrogance, haughtiness, and superiority. It's the kind of pride that Solomon referred to when he wrote:

Pride goes before destruction, and haughtiness before a fall. (Proverbs 16:18)

This is the pride that Obadiah, the next Minor Prophet we'll consider, warned about in his little book. We say "little," not to imply a miniscule message, but to describe its brevity (Obadiah is the shortest book in the Old Testament). Don't let the lack of length fool you. The book of Obadiah, small as it is, contains one of the biggest messages of the Minor Prophets.

What's the Big Deal?

So far, the first three Minor Prophets have talked about infidelity, turning away from God, and oppression. We can understand how those things would tick God off. But when it comes to pride, we have to wonder: Why does it offend God the way it does? What's wrong with having a proper sense of your own value? Nothing, but that's not what we're talking about. The pride God hates is the kind that tells Him, "Some people may need you, but I'm doing just fine, thank you." It's the kind of pride that substitutes human independence for God dependence. As James Montgomery Boice observes,

> Nothing lies so much at the heart of the problems of the human race as this prideful desire to take over God's place or, which amounts nearly to the same thing, to pretend that we can do without Him.[1]

The Pride of Satan

Pride was at the root of Satan's rebellion against God. "I will climb to the highest heavens and be like the Most High," Satan said proudly (Isaiah 14:14). Of course, God threw Satan and his demonic cohorts out of heaven, but Satan's nature didn't change. He used the same tactic to appeal to Adam and Eve. He told them that they could "become just like God, knowing everything, both good and evil" (Genesis 3:5).

Edom and Weep

We know very little about Obadiah (do you get the impression that the Minor Prophets didn't do much to promote themselves?) except that he was a prophet. Scholars aren't even sure when he wrote his book. Some say it was around 850 B.C., when the Philistines invaded Jerusalem. Other experts say it was more likely written between 605 and 586 B.C., when Babylon conquered Judah and carried off her people into captivity.

What is certain is that in both instances, the ancient kingdom of Edom—the focus of the central theme of Obadiah—was a neighbor to Judah. In both cases, Edom refused to help its neighbor in any way. More significantly, history tells us that Edom was an ally of Babylon when Jerusalem fell in 586 B.C. and participated in the plunder of the city. Even worse, the Edomites celebrated Jerusalem's destruction.

> O LORD, remember what the Edomites did on the day the armies of Babylon captured Jerusalem. "Destroy it!" they yelled. "Level it to the ground!" (Psalm 137:7)

In other words, Edom was like the looters who descend on a city that has just been through a deadly riot or a catastrophe of some kind. The Edomites may not have started the attack that destroyed Jerusalem, but they took serious advantage of their neighbor's desperate condition. It's no wonder that Obadiah begins with a prophecy that God is about to severely judge the nation of Edom.

> The LORD says, "I will cut you down to size among the nations, Edom; you will be small and despised. You are proud because you live in a rock fortress and make your home high in the mountains. 'Who can ever reach us way up here?' you ask boastfully. Don't fool yourselves! Though you soar as high as eagles and build your nest among the stars, I will bring you crashing down. I, the LORD, have spoken!" (Obadiah 2–4)

Proof of the Pride

Clearly God was ticked off at Edom. Why? Was it because the Edomites stood by and celebrated and looted while God's city was being plundered and destroyed? Well, that certainly didn't help. But notice in the verses above that God's anger and His judgment came directly from Edom's arrogance and pride. The way Edom treated Israel was merely the *proof* of the pride. The *root* of the pride went much deeper.

All About Edom

Besides being neighbors, Israel and Edom were connected in another way. The people of Israel were descended from Jacob, the son of Isaac and the grandson of Abraham. The people of Edom were descended from Esau, Jacob's twin brother. So in effect, the nations of Israel and Edom were brother nations.

God instructed Israel: "Do not detest the Edomites . . . because the Edomites are your relatives" (Deuteronomy 23:7). The same directive applied to Edom, but the Edomites paid no attention to it. If anything, the Edomites made it their business to harass Israel. For example, when the Israelites wanted to pass through Edom on their way to the Promised Land, the Edomites refused.

Edom wasn't just a lousy neighbor; it was a rotten brother as well. God doesn't like it when family members mistreat each other. It ticks Him off (Obadiah 12, 1 Timothy 5:8).

Root of the Pride

Dr. Boice offers three reasons why Edom was so proud. Don't be surprised if these sound a little familiar. God's Word is timeless.

Impressive defenses. They say the best offense is a strong defense, and Edom had one of the strongest defense systems in the ancient world. The capital city of Edom was Petra, which means "rock." Indeed, Petra was considered an impregnable fortress because it was built among towering rocky walls. The city was accessible only through a narrow, winding canyon. Along the canyon walls were thousands of ornately carved caves used as dwellings for the citizens of Petra. You can see understand why the Edomites would say, "Who can ever reach us way up here?"

Strong alliances. Even though Edom bordered Israel, it chose to side with Babylon, one of the true superpowers of the ancient world. The Edomites also allied with other lesser powers as it suited them. If ever a nation had a group of "trusted friends," it was Edom.

Renowned wisdom. The Edomites were known throughout the ancient world for their wisdom. Solomon was considered the smartest man in the world, and one of the ways his wisdom was measured was to compare it to the people of Edom (1 Kings 4:30).

From an earthly perspective, the Edomites were untouchable. From a heavenly perspective, however, Edom and its capital city were sitting ducks. Everything Edom put its faith in—its defenses, its allies, and its wisdom—caused it to openly and defiantly declare independence from God. God's pronouncement upon Edom addressed each of these three roots of pride.

> Every nook and cranny of Edom will be searched and looted.
> Every treasure will be found and taken. (Obadiah 6)

The people of Edom thought their allies would keep them secure, but just four years after the Babylonians razed Jerusalem, they returned to invade and overthrow Edom:

> All your allies will turn against you. They will help to chase you from your land. They will promise you peace, while plotting your destruction. Your trusted friends will set traps for you, and you won't even know about it. (v. 7)

The people of Edom thought their wisdom would preserve them, but God knew better:

> "At that time not a single wise person will be left in the whole land of Edom!" says the LORD. (v. 8)

What was true for Edom is true for all nations: The greater the pride, the more disastrous the fall. "All governments have been placed in power by God" (Romans 13:1). And He will bring down any nation that puts itself above God. Nothing escapes His attention.

According to Boice, the world has seen twenty-one great civilizations. "But each one has passed away in time to make room for the next. Once there was Egypt, but ancient Egypt was destroyed and that which is now Egypt is no world power. Once there was Babylon, but it too passed away. So with Greece and Rome."[2] In this century, you can add to that list the Soviet Union, a nation once full of pride and arrogance and defiance to the living God.

And what about America? There is greatness, but there is also pride. Is America completely dependent on its defenses, its alliances, and its wisdom? Sometimes it seems that way, and that's not good.

The Pride of Edom Is Our Pride

It's not enough to point the finger at any one nation, because a nation is nothing more than the sum of its people. We need to take these things personally. We need to look in the mirror and examine our own lives to see if there are any sources of pride that could lead to our own downfall.

Have we built *impressive defenses,* such as careers we think make us secure? Money experts sometimes use the word *hedge* to describe a strategy that defends one's financial position from future calamity. It's good to plan for the future, but it's a mistake to take pride in that security. Hedges mean nothing to God. Our financial security means even less if that's where we put our trust. It wasn't too long ago that people figured any investment in technology was a direct path to financial independence. Now you would stand a better chance of raising venture capital for a worm farm in Missouri than a dotcom in the Silicon Valley. How quickly things can change!

> You can have no greater sign of confirmed pride than when you think you are humble.
>
> —William Law

Have we developed *strong alliances* to certain earthly things that have no eternal value? Do we take pride in the company we work for, the neighborhood we live in, and the schools our children attend because we think these alliances make us better than everybody else? Are we so brand conscious that even the cars we drive or the clothes we wear give us a sense of superiority? These attitudes may not seem like a big deal, but God notices them. Nothing escapes His attention.

Finally, do we take too much pride in our *renowned wisdom*? Education is important, but faith in our own knowledge and learning is misplaced. Do we think we have the wisdom and the will to solve any problem, overcome any obstacle, and defeat any enemy? Placing our confidence in human intelligence alone means we are telling God that we don't really need Him. And God is willing to let us have our independence.

> Though the LORD is great, he cares for the humble, but he keeps his distance from the proud. (Psalm 138:6)

What Does God Want from Us?

Some of what God does is a mystery, but His expectations of us are not. We never have to wonder what God wants from us, because He has told us directly in His personal message to humankind, the Bible. Here's what God says about turning away from an independent spirit of pride to a dependent spirit of humility:

> Then if my people who are called by name will humble themselves and pray and seek my face and turn from their wicked ways, I will hear from heaven and will forgive their sins and heal their land. (2 Chronicles 7:14).

As we talked about in chapter 2, seeking God begins with the people of God. Blaming "godless people" for our problems is futile. We need to show the world how to live by the way we live. This isn't a mystery. We don't have to wonder what it will take to get our nation—or our families or our churches, for that matter—back into God's good graces. He has told us exactly what He wants.

God wants us to humble ourselves. If pride ticks God off, then the opposite of pride—humility—pleases Him. Humility isn't weakness.

It's admitting we can't solve all our problems alone. We need God's defense, God's alliance, and God's wisdom.

God wants us to pray. Prayer is the way we communicate with God, telling Him our deepest needs and asking for His help. "The earnest prayer of a righteous person has great power and wonderful results" (James 5:16).

God wants us to seek His face. This means adopting God's perspective on the world and its people. Pride motivates us to look down on people. God wants us to serve others.

God wants us to turn back to Him from our wicked ways. *Wicked* is such a dirty word. We're not wicked, are we? Oh yeah. God says, "The human heart is most deceitful and desperately wicked. Who really knows how bad it is? But I know!" (Jeremiah 17:9).

O Brother, Where Art Thou?

The first part of Obadiah tells us why God gets ticked off at the pride of Edom. But God isn't finished. In the second part of this short book, God explains why He will punish Edom: The people failed to help their brothers in Israel. The people of Israel and the people of Edom descended from brothers (Jacob and Esau), and they are still "close relatives" (v. 10). Relatives should help each other, but instead Edom

- deserted Israel (v. 11)
- stood aloof, refusing to help (v. 11)
- gloated when Israel was exiled (v. 12)
- rejoiced when Israel suffered misfortune (v. 12)

All of these are attitudes, and they are all extensions of pride. But pride doesn't stop with attitude. Eventually pride takes action. When you feel superior to someone else, you will inevitably take advantage of them, which is exactly why Edom

- looted Israel's homes (v. 13)
- killed those who tried to escape (v. 14)
- handed the survivors over to their enemies (v. 14)

It's an ugly progression, but it's not unprecedented. Remember the first brothers, Cain and Abel? When God accepted Abel's offerings over Cain's offerings, Cain's pride was hurt, and he became angry. God warned him about allowing his pride to turn into action:

> You will be accepted if you respond in the right way. But if you refuse to respond correctly, then watch out! Sin is waiting to attack and destroy you, and you must subdue it. (Genesis 4:7)

Cain didn't listen to God's advice. He allowed his attitude of pride to fill and subdue him. As a result, Cain killed Abel. When God asked Cain, "Where is your brother?" Cain replied:

> Am I my brother's keeper? (Genesis 4:9 KJV)

It's the age-old question. If God had asked the Edomites where the people of Israel were, they would have answered the same way. In reality, the people of Edom didn't have to answer—the answer was in their actions. They didn't think they had to care for their neighbors and brothers, but they were wrong. God expected Edom to care for Israel in its misfortune and to weep when Israel suffered.

There's a strong principle of brotherhood here, and we don't think we're stretching things too far to apply the same principles to all of us today in at least three different arenas.

The brotherhood of humanity. As human beings sharing the same planet with other human beings, we have a responsibility to care for our brothers. The world is a big place filled with more than 6 billion people, and many of them are hurting, hungry, and harassed. It can become discouraging to think about the incredible needs "out there," but don't let your discouragement lead to inaction. You can't do everything, but you can do something. Give blood to the Red Cross. Send checks to World Vision. Build houses for Habitat for Humanity. Don't just sit there—do *something*.

At the same time, don't get so focused on the bigger needs of our world that you forget about your own neighborhood. There are hurting people who need your touch and your encouragement. Jesus said that the second greatest commandment is: "Love your neighbor as yourself" (Matthew 22:39). This applies to neighbors everywhere, but it starts with the people next door.

The brotherhood of brothers. Isn't it amazing how many families get into real-life family feuds? It isn't just brothers fighting with brothers, but husbands fighting with wives and children fighting with parents. God designed the family to be a place of sanctuary and comfort, a shelter in the time of storm. The family is a place where a husband should love his wife, and a wife should respect her husband. A family should be a place where parents encourage their children, and children honor their parents. For brotherhood to have any value outside of the family, the family is where it needs to begin.

The brotherhood of believers. There's an old saying that the church is the only place where people shoot their wounded. When a believer gets into trouble, we gossip rather than help (disguised as "Christian concern," of course). Rather than comforting a fallen brother, we criticize—usually to other people. What a terrible witness to the world! We need to repent of these actions and heed the words of Paul:

> Don't just pretend that you love others. Really love them. Hate what is wrong. Stand on the side of the good. Love each other with genuine affection, and take delight in honoring each other. (Romans 12:9–10)

The Apple of God's Eye

If there's a consistent theme running through the Minor Prophets, it's that God will one day restore the nation of Israel. Clearly, Israel is important to God. The Jews are His chosen people. Kay Arthur wrote: "God said that whoever touched Israel touched the apple of his eye."[3] God promised Abraham that He would: "bless those who bless you and curse those who curse you" (Genesis 12:3). There's no question that Edom cursed Israel, motivating God to curse Edom. On the flip side, nations throughout history who have been friends and protectors to Israel have been blessed.

God Protects His People

Throughout the Bible, God expresses His concern for the oppressed. Even more, God is a champion of the downtrodden.

> For he has not ignored the suffering of the needy. He has not turned and walked away. He has listened to their cries for help. (Psalm 22:24)

So why is the world still full of hunger and suffering and oppression? Because God isn't done yet. The world isn't the way it's supposed to be because God hasn't finished His work. But a time is coming when God will make everything right. That's the message of the third and final part of Obadiah.

First, the oppressors and those like Edom—people and nations filled with the kind of pride that keeps them from knowing God—will be overthrown and judged:

> The day is near when I, the LORD, will judge the godless nations! As you have done to Israel, so it will be done to you. All your evil deeds will fall back on your own heads. (Obadiah 15)

Then, God's people will be restored:

> But Jerusalem will become a refuge for those who escape; it will be a holy place. And the people of Israel will come back to reclaim their inheritance. (v. 17)

Obadiah begins his book with the somber declaration that God is the judge, and he ends it with the joyous announcement that "the LORD himself will be king!" (v. 21). As a child of God, you can take comfort in knowing this about God. Yes, pride ticks Him off. And He is the God of justice who has every right to judge every person and every nation on earth. But He is also the God of love who gives hope to the hopeless, healing to the hurting, and comfort to the brokenhearted. Most of all, he protects those who call out to Him. As Jesus said:

> God blesses those who realize their need for him,
>   for the Kingdom of Heaven is given to them.
>   (Matthew 5:3)

5

YOU CAN RUN,
BUT YOU CAN'T HIDE

With four chapters of this book already under your belt (or wherever you put them), a few things about God should be embedded in the soft tissue of your cranium.

First, God isn't absent-minded when it comes to His creation. He didn't construct the world and then forget all about it, like a child who quickly tires of playing with the new birthday toys and then amuses himself with the discarded boxes and wrapping paper.

Second, God isn't so preoccupied with the rest of the universe that He has no time to spare for humanity. Unlike a wealthy absentee landlord who owns an apartment building but never checks on it because his other financial deals are more pressing, God is continually focused on the tenants of Planet Earth.

And third, God doesn't just stare at what's happening down here without getting personally involved. We aren't like one of those ant farms—God didn't sandwich the world between two pieces of celestial glass and then set us on a shelf to amuse Himself by watching as we crawl through life. As we have seen from the messages of Hosea, Joel, Amos, and Obadiah, there are times when God sees that we are digging in the wrong direction, and it ticks Him off. Then He is compelled to grab the world and shake us up a bit.

The shaking we have seen so far has always been on a national level. For example, Hosea and Amos gave their warnings to the northern kingdom of Israel; Amos preached in the southern kingdom of Judah; and the message of Obadiah was directed in the nation of Edom. If you stopped reading the Minor Prophets after these four, you might get the idea that God only gets ticked off at nations and kingdoms, or that He imposes His discipline against the empire as a whole but never on a single individual.

After all, is it reasonable to think that God bothers to care—or even know—about the private, particular details of your personal behavior? Aren't you just one, teensy-weensy, insignificant ant in an overpopulated colony? Isn't it possible that you could escape personalized judgment because God's view of you is obscured by a smudge on the glass? These aren't difficult questions to answer. If you've ever taken the time to watch a single ant scurry across a picnic table, just remember what you did to that ant just before it crawled up the side of your cupcake.

God's sovereign control and participation in the course of nations does not preoccupy or distract Him from involvement in our individual lives. To the contrary, God is concerned with governments, kingdoms, and empires *because* they are comprised of individuals, each of whom is loved by God. God often works at the *macro* level (that would be with nations), but He is always involved at the *micro* level (that would be with you).

The macro and micro activities of God are best illustrated in the life of Jonah (who is the only Minor Prophet that has a respectable public-recognition rating). As with all of the Minor Prophets, Jonah delivered a message of how God wanted to deal with a group of people; in this case, the citizens of Nineveh. So, like the other prophets, Jonah's message was important. But unlike the other prophets:

- Jonah was the only one who rejected his commission as a prophet of God,
- he was the only prophet who tried to conceal his message, and
- reading the words of his message (there are only eight) is not as revealing as examining his behavior.

God used the circumstances in the life of Hosea to illustrate a message. But it was different with Jonah. Hosea walked in obedience to God. Jonah, on the other hand, was running away from God. And that was the problem, because . . .

GOD IS TICKED OFF WHEN WE ARE HEADED IN THE WRONG DIRECTION

A Whale of a Story

Most of the books of the Minor Prophets give an overview of the message and events of their ministries that spanned decades. With the Book of Jonah, all we get is the narrative account of one of Jonah's prophetic assignments. (He probably had more, but only one adventure is covered in the brief forty-eight verses of this story.)

Before we get to the specifics of his story (which you think you already know) a little background may be helpful. Jonah lived in Gath-hepher. It was a little town about three miles north of Nazareth in lower Galilee. This means that Jonah was a prophet in the northern kingdom Israel. His story takes place at least thirty years before Assyria invaded Israel in 722 B.C.

Economically, things were going well for Israel. Spiritually, they were going down the drain. But that wasn't Jonah's problem. God had given the assignment of Israel's condition to Jonah's compadres (guys like Amos and Hosea). Jonah must have drawn the short straw because he had a much harder assignment: to preach to the people of Nineveh, the capital city of Assyria.

Assyria was Israel's most dreaded enemy. The Assyrian empire was known worldwide for its brutality, and they were the most feared of all nations. Nineveh was the epicenter of this evil empire.

Tarshish Wasn't the End of the World, but You Could See It from There

Every time a Minor Prophet was told to speak out against a hostile, foreign nation, he got to do so from the safety of his own home. Except for Jonah. He was told to preach his message of God's judgment on the enemy's turf:

> The LORD gave this message to Jonah son of Amittai: "Get up and go to the great city of Nineveh! Announce my judgment against it because I have seen how wicked its people are." (Jonah 1:1–2)

Nineveh was five hundred miles northeast of Jonah's hometown of Gath-hepher. So, Jonah immediately booked a trip—to Tarshish, a coastal city two thousand miles to the *west*, absolutely as far away from Nineveh as Jonah could go.

What Made Jonah Run?

There is no evidence that Jonah argued with God about his assignment. He just took off in the opposite direction. Why? As we'll discuss a little later in this chapter, Jonah didn't want God to give His blessings and grace to a pagan nation. He didn't want the Assyrians to respond and repent, and thereby be spared. Everyone knew that the Ninevites were a wicked people. Beyond that, however, it is possible that Jonah had heard the message preached by Amos that Assyria was going to invade and obliterate Israel. He didn't want to share God's grace with an enemy that was going to conquer his own nation.

But Jonah didn't just refuse to budge. He actually fled. So we suspect that Jonah was also a little jumpy. Since Nineveh was known for its merciless violence, Jonah must have feared for his personal safety. The potential for danger probably scared the prophecy out of him.

At the seaport of Joppa, Jonah boarded a ship that was sailing to Tarshish. It wasn't long before a violent storm threatened to sink the ship. The sailors asked everyone to pray to whatever god they believed in, and they started throwing cargo overboard to lighten the load. The captain found Jonah asleep in the bottom of the ship and made him join the prayer vigil. The sailors tossed dice to determine if someone was bad luck, and Jonah's number came up. Whether he was sacrificially heroic, or just suicidally fatalistic, Jonah confessed that he was running from the Lord, and he persuaded the sailors to throw him overboard. As soon as they did, the storm subsided.

It Must Have Been Someone I Ate

Jonah must have figured that life was over as the waves overpowered him. But God wasn't finished:

Now the LORD had arranged for a great fish to swallow Jonah. And Jonah was inside the fish for three days and three nights. (1:17)

Have you ever looked for an atmosphere or an environment that was conducive to prayer? Well, Jonah found that it was very easy to pray from the inside of a fish's stomach. Oh, sure, there were lots of jerky motions, and seaweed and ocean debris kept slapping him in the face, not to mention how bad the place must have smelt (pun intended). Despite those distractions, the constant confrontation of death was a pretty good motivator for prayer.

Excerpts from his prayers can be found in Jonah 2:2–9. They read like something from the Psalms:

> I sank beneath the waves, and death was very near. The waters closed in around me, and seaweed wrapped itself around my head. I sank down to the very roots of the mountains. I was locked out of life and imprisoned in the land of the dead. But you, O LORD my God, have snatched me from the yawning jaws of death! (2:5–6)

In order to make Jonah realize his sin of rebellion, God had to take him to the depths, literally. God wanted Jonah to acknowledge that He was the sole source of life. It happened when Jonah cried out, "For my salvation comes from the LORD alone" (2:9).

> Then the LORD ordered the fish to spit up Jonah on the beach, and it did. (2:10)

But Sackcloth Is So Scratchy

Jonah didn't have long to wonder if God had fired him from his prophet's job. Jonah was still dripping wet when God reiterated the original assignment:

> Then the LORD spoke to Jonah a second time: "Get up and go to the great city of Nineveh, and deliver the message of judgment I have given you." (3:1–2)

Just as before, when Jonah heard those words he started running. But this time he ran straight toward Nineveh. (It was a five-hundred-mile trek, so we're sure he walked part of the way.)

As soon as he entered the city gates, Jonah started shouting his message, and he kept at it during the three days it took him to walk the thirty-six-mile distance through the center of the city. The Bible only records eight words of what he said, but you can see that they communicated the essential point of his message:

> Forty days from now Nineveh will be destroyed! (3:4)

In Luke 11:30, Jesus said that what happened to Jonah was a sign to the people of Nineveh. It is likely that this "sign" was his appearance. His skin was probably splotchy and permanently bleached from the acids and fluids in the stomach of the fish. Not only was he proclaiming a message of doom, he probably had the appearance of a ghost.

Could It Really Happen?

In his book *The Harmony of Science and Scripture,* Dr. Harry Rimmer reported the story of an English sailor who fell overboard and was swallowed by a fish. After a day or two, the fish was seen floating on the surface of the water. Sailors pulled the fish to shore and filleted it, only to find their shipmate alive. Years later, Dr. Rimmer interviewed this sailor and verified that his skin had a permanent chalky-white color to it. (Reports that the sailor had a constant craving for tartar sauce have not been verified.)

Sermons don't have to be long to be effective. Jonah's brief message produced the greatest evangelistic response in history:

> The people of Nineveh believed God's message, and from the greatest to the least, they decided to go without food and wear sackcloth to show their sorrow. . . . Then the king and his nobles sent this decree throughout the city . . . "Everyone is required to wear sackcloth and pray earnestly to God. Everyone must turn from their evil ways and stop all their violence. Who can tell? Perhaps even yet God will have pity on us and hold back his fierce anger from destroying us." (3:5, 7–9)

Most of the Minor Prophets tell a story that goes something like this: (a) The people are living in a manner that ticks God off; (b) God sends them a warning; (c) the people ignore the warning; so (d) God administers judgment. While (a) and (b) are the same in this case, the rest of Jonah's story has a happy ending:

> When God saw that they had put a stop to their evil ways, he had mercy on them and didn't carry out the destruction he had threatened. (3:10)

We're sure that you have heard the adventure of Jonah before, but perhaps this is where you thought the story ended. Surprise! The story isn't over yet. It peaks at the end of chapter 3 with the display of God's forgiveness and grace toward the city of Nineveh, but an additional chapter is required because Jonah needs another attitude adjustment.

Jonah Has It Made in the Shade

Jonah was happy when God was ticked off at Nineveh. But he didn't like the fact that God spared the city in response to Nineveh's repentance. Now it was Jonah's turn to be ticked off:

> This change of plans upset Jonah, and he became very angry. So he complained to the LORD about it: "Didn't I say before I left home that you would do this, LORD? That is why I ran away to Tarshish! I knew that you were a gracious and compassionate God, slow to get angry and filled with unfailing love. I knew how easily you could cancel your plans for destroying these people. (4:1–2)

There sat Jonah on a hillside in the hot Assyrian sun, overlooking the city of Nineveh. He was pouting because God had shown mercy to Israel's archenemy. To teach Jonah a lesson, God caused a gigantic plant to grow up overnight so that Jonah had shade the next day. He could now pout in comfort. But then God caused a worm to eat away at the plant. It shriveled away and the shade was gone. To make Jonah's discomfort worse, God caused a scorching desert wind to blow. He got so mad and miserable that he wanted to die.

When God had Jonah at the breaking point, He zapped him with this truth: Jonah cared more about the plant than the people of Nineveh. In God's paradigm, those people were important. Because God loved them, so should Jonah.

It's Not about the Fish

The story of Jonah is often categorized with folk tales and urban legends. Jonah gets lumped together with Johnny Appleseed, Paul Bunyan, and Rip Van Winkle. With the exception of the creation account in Genesis 1, no part of the Bible seems to generate as much skepticism as the Book of Jonah. Critics are so hung up on the story of a big fish and the other details that they miss the point about a big God. (Could a fish really swallow a man? Could a man really survive for three days on the inside of a fish?)

We don't find these questions—or others like them—to be sufficient reason to doubt the reality of the Jonah account. After all, God created the entire universe, so we don't think it strains a brain to believe that He could accomplish the miracle reported in the Book of Jonah. Because God is supernatural, He can do things that are beyond the traditional notions of "nature." It's an omnipotence thing.

But Jesus is perhaps the strongest evidence of the truth of the Jonah story. Jesus used the period of Jonah's "burial" in the belly of the fish as a sign of the number of days He would spend in the grave:

> One day some teachers of religious law and Pharisees came to Jesus and said, "Teacher, we want you to show us a miraculous sign to prove that you are from God."
>
> But Jesus replied, "The only sign I will give . . . is the sign of the prophet Jonah. For as Jonah was in the belly of the great fish for three days and three nights, so I, the Son of Man, will be in the heart of the earth for three days and three nights." (Matthew 12:38–40)

We think it is extremely doubtful that Jesus would refer to His death and resurrection by making reference to a folk tale.

The Macro

The typical analysis of the Book of Jonah involves a look at the micro—Jonah. But before we go there, let's not lose sight of the macro perspective. As with the other Minor Prophets, the Book of Jonah shows how God deals with a group of people. This time, however, those people are non-Jews, and they repent and receive God's favor. As such, more than any other Old Testament book, Jonah stands for the proposition that God has a plan of redemption for all people, not just the Jews. Here are a few specific points that should not escape our macro examination:

God's kindness toward the Ninevites is shown by the fact that He sent a prophet to them. Instead of simply wiping these utterly corrupt people off the map, God confronted them with their wickedness and warned them of the consequences. It was God's grace that gave them a chance to repent.

God kept after Jonah to make sure that the message got delivered. He didn't get distracted or let Jonah off the hook after the fish business. God was intent upon getting His message to the people of Nineveh.

God sent Jonah into the city. In his tirade against Israel, Amos listed God's complaints against the neighboring nations, but he didn't even tiptoe across the border to whisper this message of impending doom. Here, God had Jonah walk through the center of the city to proclaim His message, making sure that it reached the ears of every resident.

There was a lesson for the nation of Israel in all of this. The great result of Jonah's prophecy was the repentance of the pagan city of Nineveh. Israel was God's chosen people, yet they had turned a deaf ear to God with their spiritual compromises and idolatry. But the pagan nation believed in God when it heard the message.

And Now for the Micro

Let's spend the rest of this chapter examining the personal lessons that can be learned from the life of Jonah. He is representative of all of us. The manner in which God dealt with him is the same manner God may choose to use with us (except no great fish is likely to be involved). From the outset, Jonah knew two things:

- The power of God's message—Jonah knew that the people of Nineveh would respond to God's conviction.
- The forgiveness in God's nature—he knew God would forgive and bless the Ninevites if they repented from their sins and worshiped God.

These were important things for him to know, but his theological knowledge was limited to the macro stage. He knew how God dealt with kingdoms and nations, but nothing about microtheology. He didn't know the ways in which he, personally, could offend God.

GOD IS TICKED OFF WHEN WE AREN'T GOING IN THE RIGHT DIRECTION

The life of Jonah makes this obvious. When God tells us to go one way and we run defiantly in the opposite direction, He is displeased. But sometimes we aren't going in the right direction, and it has nothing to do with our actions. In those times, like Jonah sitting on the hillside, it is all about our attitude.

Fleeting Feet: When We Are Running Away from Him

It is easy to see the mistake Jonah made. He disobeyed God by going in the wrong direction. The more fascinating part of the story, however, is the manner in which God dealt with his disobedience.

God continued to work in the circumstances of Jonah's life. Jonah was trying to run away from God, but he couldn't escape God's sovereignty. Jonah ran, but God pursued. God prepared the storm, and He prepared the fish. Those things didn't just happen. Jonah was the only part of God's plan that failed, and God had even made a provision for that.

God wouldn't let Jonah forget Him. Part of God's plan included surrounding Jonah with those spiritually sensitive sailors. They actually forced Jonah to audibly recite his connection with the God he was trying to forget. According to Jonah 1:7–10, the shipboard inquisition went something like this:

Sailors: Where are you from?
Jonah: Israel.

Sailors: Who are your people?

Jonah: The Jews.

Sailors: What do you do?

Jonah: I am a prophet of the Lord God
Almighty, the Creator of the sky and the sea.

It is hard to forget about God after you have said all of that. God kindly put Jonah in a situation in which he was reminded of the things he had previously professed to believe.

When Jonah was finally willing to obey, God was ready to use him. Jonah defied God by running in the opposite direction—the *wrong* direction. Jonah's path got him into deep trouble, and God let him get in over his head. But when he recognized that God's direction was the only course for salvation, then God bailed him out.

God will deal with us in the same way if we try to run away from Him. He may let us go; He may even arrange for a boat to take us in the opposite direction. But sooner or later, God is going to bring storms into our lives. Why? Because He loves us and knows that traveling to Tarshish in rebellion is not in our best interests.

So, if you feel as though you are drowning and you know it is because you've been running from God, then call out to Him. He is there, ready to have you belched up onto dry land. As Jonah said, "Salvation comes from the LORD alone" (2:9). He may keep you under water until you can say it and mean it.

Hardened Heart: When We Aren't Walking with Him

At the end of his story, Jonah wasn't running from God. He just wasn't walking with Him. And that ticked God off too. Because he was a Jew, Jonah held a privileged position as one of God's chosen people. Like an only child who doesn't want to share his parents' love with a newborn sibling, Jonah didn't want to see the people of Nineveh receive God's forgiveness. He was guilty of feeling spiritually superior. He wanted exclusive rights to God and wasn't willing to share that with anyone who wasn't a Jew. This meant that Jonah didn't share the sentiments of God's heart.

If we are honest with ourselves, there are times when our attitudes toward others are distorted. There are times when we lack spiritual sympathy for certain people. Although God gave us what we needed (salvation) instead of what we deserved (judgment), we want Him to give these people what they deserve instead of what they need. Like Jonah, we have an attitude of spiritual superiority.

> The great merit of the book [of Jonah] is that it comments objectively on the human scene, especially the religious side of it, from the divine viewpoint. Here lies the secret of the book's continuing fascination, for readers see an aspect of self in its compelling story. What one makes of it will depend partly on self-understanding and partly on one's grasp of the all-embracing love of the God we serve.
>
> —Joyce Baldwin

Now, let's get a little more personal. Are you less than excited that God wants to save certain people? What about the person at work who has embarrassed and ridiculed you for your faith? Or what if there was a criminal who raped your daughter or shot your son? Or suppose there was a militant foreign leader who was dedicated to the destruction of America. In light of the events of the terrorist attacks on September 11, 2001, this is not difficult to imagine. Would you be more interested in seeing God's love or judgment poured out on that man?

In any of these cases, would you want this person to suffer, or would you rejoice if he turned to God and received His salvation and blessings? Your answer to that question will give you a good idea of whether or not you are walking with God.

Hook, Line, and Sinker

Neither of us likes to fish. We don't really see the sport or the fun in it. As far as we're concerned, fishing is just a jerk at one end of the line waiting for a jerk at the other end. It seems such a laborious way to take it easy.

But we do have a lot of friends who are fishermen. (At least they were friends until they read the preceding paragraph.) Based on our conversations with them, it seems that fishing stimulates the brain, because it seems to give our friends very vivid imaginations and an unrestrained compulsion to exaggerate.

As we get ready to leave the world's greatest fish story, we want to make sure that our brains aren't adversely affected by imagination or exaggeration. So let's forget about the fish for a moment. The story of Jonah is not about a fish. And it's not about the people of Nineveh. It's not even about Jonah. The story we have been studying is all about the heart of God.

As you continue to read the messages of the remaining seven Minor Prophets, you'll hear again how God deals with nations and kingdoms. That's the macro perspective. But don't ever forget that His concern for the macro is premised on a microperspective: you!

We've come up with the following seven principles from the story of Jonah that reveal how God is actively involved in your life.

1. God's care for you continues even when you defy His call.
2. There is no limit to what God will do to get your attention if you are trying to ignore Him.
3. If you are planning to run away from God, there will likely be some disruptions in your travel plans.
4. Sometimes it takes physical deliverance to prompt spiritual renewal.
5. You can be more effective in sharing God's message of grace and redemption when you have experienced it for yourself.
6. All of God's resources in creation are available for His purposes in caring for you.
7. The condition of your heart is as important as the location of your feet.

We are sure that we missed a few. Read the forty-eight verses of Jonah and add to the list.

WHAT DOES GOD REQUIRE OF US?

C an you imagine any job more thankless and discouraging than that of a prophet of God? We tried to come up with some current examples and we couldn't think of anything that even comes close (with the possible exception of being a lawyer). The role of the Old Testament prophet was the most unusual and most difficult job ever conceived by God or man.

Don't be fooled by certain people running around today who call themselves prophets or messengers of God. They don't even come close to the real deal. For one thing, some of these fakes live the life of luxury and minor celebrity simply because they've duped enough people into believing they are genuine. Other people don't necessarily call themselves prophets, but instead claim to have a direct link to God that nobody else has. It's amazing how many of these charlatans manage to get their own television shows on cable.

Besides being poor imitations of the real thing, these false prophets fall flat on their collective faces in one very important category: accuracy. You see, by definition, a true prophet of God can never be wrong, because as a messenger of God, he must reflect God's character and perfection. In the Old Testament, if anyone claiming to be a prophet made a wrong prediction, even one, he would be put to death (Deuteronomy 18:20–22). And you thought you worked in a high-risk environment!

Convincing prophets to take the job must have been a real challenge. Imagine a recruiting advertisement in the "Help Wanted" section of the Jerusalem Gazette:

Help Wanted

Position open for prophet of God. Must be willing to work long hours with no overtime pay. In fact, there is no pay whatsoever. Also, no paid vacation, no retirement plan, and no insurance. Self-defense certification not necessary, but recommended. Anointing by the Almighty highly recommended.

The Life of a Prophet

So what was it like to be a prophet? Like we said, it was thankless and discouraging, mainly because people rarely responded to the prophet's words. Maybe if the prophets had stuck to predicting future events (known as "foretelling"), the people would have found them mildly interesting. But much of what the prophets did involved protesting current activities (known simply as "telling"), such as idolatry, corruption, and injustice. People today don't like to hear preachers ragging on them for their evil ways. The citizens of Israel back in the days of the prophets weren't any different.

Page from a Prophet's Diary

In addition to the unpopular nature of their messages, the prophets didn't always understand their own words, so you can imagine a little frustration setting in. Here's a page from the diary of Jeremiah, who answered God's help-wanted ad:

O LORD, you persuaded me, and I allowed myself to be persuaded. You are stronger than I am, and you overpowered me. Now I am mocked by everyone in the city. Whenever I speak, the words come out in a violent outburst. . . . So these messages from the LORD have made me a household joke. And I can't stop! If I say I'll never mention the LORD or speak in his name, his word burns in my heart like a fire. It's like a fire in my bones! I am weary of holding it in!

I have heard the many rumors about me. . . . Even my old

friends are watching me, waiting for a fatal slip. "He will trap himself," they say, "and then we will get our revenge on him." (Jeremiah 20:7–10)

What a life! Even their friends turned against them. But it was a life the prophets lived willingly. Despite the discouragement that often afflicted them, they were faithful to God. Why? Because God had promised to stand with them. Here's another section from Jeremiah's journal. Let this be an encouragement to you the next time you feel ridiculed:

> But the LORD stands beside me like a great warrior. Before him they will stumble. They cannot defeat me. They will be shamed and thoroughly humiliated. Their dishonor will never be forgotten. O LORD Almighty! You know those who are righteous, and you examine the deepest thoughts of hearts and minds. Let me see your vengeance against them, for I have committed my cause to you. (Jeremiah 20:11–12)

Reason for Hope

Not everything was doom and gloom for the prophets. Occasionally the people listened and turned back to God, if only for a while. And sometimes God gave the prophet a glimpse into a future world of peace that would be ruled by the coming Messiah, the Prince of Peace.

Just like the first five prophets in our study, Micah delivered a series of warnings to God's people, only his went both to the northern kingdom of Israel and the southern kingdom of Judah during the reigns of Jotham, Ahaz, and Hezekiah (from 742 to 687 B.C.). True to form, Israel didn't listen to the prophet, and Assyrian invaders, led by Sennacherib, destroyed the capital city of Samaria in 722 B.C.

But the people of Judah, led by King Hezekiah did listen, and they did what Micah asked. Here's the historical record:

> Hezekiah son of Ahaz began to rule over Judah in the third year of King Hoshea's reign in Israel. He was twenty-five years old when he became king, and he reigned in Jerusalem

.twenty-nine years. . . . He did what was pleasing in the LORD's sight, just as his ancestor David had done. . . . There was never another king like him in the land of Judah, either before or after his time. He remained faithful to the LORD in everything. . . . so the LORD was with him, and Hezekiah was successful in everything he did. He revolted against the king of Assyria and refused to pay him tribute. He also conquered the Philistines . . . from their smallest outpost to their largest walled city. (2 Kings 18:1–3, 5–8)

Benefits to Blessing

If you have ever wondered whether obeying God has any practical benefits, take a cue from the story of King Hezekiah. Here was a young man who followed God's commands as outlined in His Word. Because he was a king, God blessed Hezekiah in a kingly fashion: He protected Judah from invading Assyrians and gave Hezekiah success as he set out to conquer the dreaded Philistines. You may not be the king of anything, but you can believe that God will bless you in practical ways if you follow His commands.

So Who Was Micah?

King Hezekiah and his people may have reaped the benefits of blessing, but it was Micah who persuaded the young ruler to do "what was pleasing in the LORD's sight." So who was this guy, and why did Hezekiah listen to him? It wasn't because Micah was a big-time prophet from the big city. He was a country boy from a little town, and when he arrived to deliver his prophecies in the capital city of Jerusalem, a well-known prophet by the name of Isaiah was already there. In fact, it was Isaiah who delivered Micah's message to King Hezekiah.

Micah was an insignificant person from the world's perspective, yet God used him in two significant ways.

God used Micah to convince the king of Judah to obey God. King Hezekiah's obedience and submission to God resulted in a revival among the people and a time of peace for the southern kingdom of Judah. While the northern kingdom of Israel was falling to Assyria, Judah enjoyed God's protection. Furthermore, God enabled the nation to subdue its enemies.

God used Micah to announce the King of kings to the world. God chose Micah to deliver a prophecy concerning the coming of the Messiah, Jesus Christ, the Prince of Peace:

> But you, O Bethlehem Ephrathah, are only a small village in Judah. Yet a ruler of Israel will come from you, one whose origins are from the distant past. . . . And he will stand to lead his flock with the LORD's strength, in the majesty of the name of the LORD his God. Then his people will live there undisturbed, for he will be highly honored all around the world. And he will be the source of our peace. (Micah 5:2, 4–5)

Six hundred years after Micah wrote those words, King Herod, a descendent of the Edomites and the ruler of Israel by order of the Roman Empire, heard about a baby boy born in the town of Bethlehem in Judea. Dignitaries had come from far away to pay tribute to this baby, who had been named Jesus. "Where is the newborn king of the Jews?" they asked (Matthew 2:2). The Bible says that Herod was deeply disturbed by this question, so he called for a meeting of the religious leaders, and he asked them, "Where did the prophets say the Messiah would be born?" Without missing a beat, they quoted the prophet Micah (Matthew 2:4–6).

Becoming a Person of Influence

Everybody wants to have influence these days. Books outlining the seventeen ways to make friends and influence people top the bestsellers list. There's nothing wrong with studying ways to become a person of influence, but before we set out to lead a company or start something new, shouldn't we find out what it takes to become a person of influence for God?

God may not have plans for you to become the next Bill Gates or the successor to Billy Graham. Few people have that kind of influence. But don't count yourself out. Look at simple Micah, the country rube. His message to King Hezekiah got the attention of a nation, and his announcement about the coming Messiah got the attention of the world. How did Micah do it?

There are at least two qualities about Micah that helped bring about his incredible influence, both of which are powerful principles we can apply today.

Micah Identified with the People

Too many Christians fall into the trap of openly and maliciously criticizing people or groups of people for their views and lifestyles. This wasn't Micah's style. Even though he condemned the sin, he didn't condemn the sinner. That's never the job of a person who claims to speak God's truth. Jesus said: "God did not send his Son into the world to condemn it, but to save it" (John 3:17). If the Son of God didn't condemn people, who do we think we are?

Besides, we're all sinners! Micah knew this, which is why he identified with the people. He had great concern and compassion for his neighbors, and he wanted to show them that he cared about what was coming if they didn't turn back to God. So he identified with them in the best way he could.

> Because of all this, I will mourn and lament. I will walk around naked and barefoot in sorrow and shame. I will howl like a jackal and wail like an ostrich. For my people's wound is far too deep to heal. It has reached into Judah, even to the gates of Jerusalem. (Micah 1:8–9)

Now, we're not suggesting that you get naked and yell like a jackal in order to identify with the people around you who have turned their backs on God. But you may have to do something nearly as humbling, such as visiting an AIDS patient, or giving an ex-gang member a job in your company, or simply inviting your neighbor to church. We may think that we have all the reasons for why people should turn to God, and we may be able to articulate them very persuasively. But if we aren't willing to identify with people at the deepest level of their need, then our words are empty.

The teaching of the apostle Paul is instructive for us. Certainly Micah would have known what he was talking about:

> If I had the gift of prophecy, and if I knew all the mysteries of the future and knew everything about everything, but didn't love others, what good would I be? (1 Corinthians 13:2)

> More people have been won by honey than by thunder.
> —James Montgomery Boice

Micah Did Not Give Up

The second quality that helped Micah become a person of influence was perseverance. This shouldn't come as a surprise. As much as we'd like Him to, God doesn't act according to our timetables. He doesn't answer prayers as promptly as we would like, He doesn't change the hearts of people we love as soon as we would like, and He hasn't corrected the world's evils as quickly as we would like.

Micah knew this about God, which is why he waited patiently for the results. He stayed on task for at least twenty years, and maybe for as long as thirty-five years. We know this because the Bible says that Micah gave the Lord's messages "during the years when Jotham, Ahaz, and Hezekiah were kings of Judah" (1:1). Historical records tell us that Jotham became king in 750 B.C., followed by Ahaz in 735 B.C., and Hezekiah in 715 B.C. Talk about perseverance! We get frustrated when we can't pull up our e-mail in less than thirty seconds.

We need to learn from the lesson of Micah's life. God does not operate according to our timetables. He is not moved by our impatience. God knows what's best, and He does things according to His schedule, not ours. If we are doing God's work, we need to trust God for the results. Again, Paul's words ring true for us today:

> So don't get tired of doing what is good. Don't get discouraged and give up, for we will reap a harvest of blessing at the appropriate time. (Galatians 6:9)

A Fresno Story of Perseverance

We occasionally make fun of Fresno, like the time we said in one of our books that the city motto is: "We live here so you don't have to." But there is a serious side to Fresno that we are very proud of. In fact, in the context of Micah and his perseverance, Fresno stands very tall. In the early 1960s, the Billy Graham Crusade came to Fresno, and many people committed their lives to Jesus Christ. Yet the city didn't change much, so two young pastors began to pray for revival.

The two pastors—and many others who caught their vision—continued to pray through the years. Their churches grew, and so did their spirit of compassion and concern. For a while it looked as if things were getting worse rather than better, as Fresno became overrun with crime and gang activity in the 1980s and early 1990s. The two pastors didn't get discouraged. In fact, they acted with courage and formed a nondenominational, interfaith fellowship designed to build the city for God. Without fanfare, civic leaders, elected officials, ministry leaders, and pastors met monthly to pray for Fresno.

Then it happened. As the millennium came to a close, a committee of concerned Christians invited Billy Graham to return to Fresno for a crusade. In the fall of 2001, nearly forty years after the two young pastors began to pray, Billy Graham came back to Fresno. Attendance records at Bulldog Stadium were broken as 200,000 people (that's half the population of the entire city) came to hear the life-changing message of Jesus Christ. How did this happen? Clearly, God responded to the faithfulness and perseverance of a few people who prayed tirelessly and did not give up.

What Ticks God Off

Here we are, halfway through the chapter, and we haven't yet told you what ticks God off. Don't worry, we haven't forgotten. It's just that Micah takes a while to get to it, but once he does, the message comes through loud and clear. These are the things that caused God to bring judgment upon Israel, and they are as contemporary and applicable as anything you'll find in the Minor Prophets.

GOD IS TICKED OFF BY FALSE TEACHING

First, God addresses the spiritual leaders, the ones who are "supposed to know right from wrong" (Micah 3:1). Instead, they are "the very ones who hate good and love evil" (3:2). God himself addresses these "false prophets":

> You are leading my people astray! You promise peace for those who give you food, but you declare war on anyone who refuses to pay you. Now the night will close around you, cutting off all your visions. Darkness will cover you, making it impossible for you to predict the future. The sun will set for you prophets, and your day will come to an end. (3:5–6)

God really doesn't like it when people who should know better—and who claim to be prophets of God or teachers of His Word—deliberately lead people astray. It ticks Him off. Jesus reinforced the consequences for those who lead others astray in the name of God when He said:

> But if anyone causes one of these little ones who trusts in me to lose faith, it would be better for that person to be thrown into the sea with a large millstone tied around the neck. . . . Temptation to do wrong is inevitable, but how terrible it will be for the person who does the tempting. (Matthew 18:6–7)

Of course, it takes two to tango. A false teacher will be successful only if he has a willing audience. Micah found this to be true with the people of Judah:

> Suppose a prophet full of lies were to say to you, "I'll preach to you the joys of wine and drink!" That's just the kind of prophet you would like! (2:11)

Unfortunately, there are false teachers out there who will prey on hapless victims (usually for money). We shouldn't be surprised. God will deal with them in His way and in His time. But that doesn't let the rest of us off the hook. False teachers are able to worm their way in because people don't know the truth. It's our responsibility to discern right from wrong. Work hard so God can approve you as one who does not need to be ashamed and who correctly explains the word of truth (2 Timothy 2:15).

GOD IS TICKED OFF BY INJUSTICE

Micah points out another major irritant to God: injustice. And it comes from the people who should know better:

> Listen to me, you leaders of Israel! You hate justice and twist all that is right. You are building Jerusalem on a foundation of murder and corruption. (3:9–10)

Injustice has always been a thorn in God's side, whether it comes from the church or the state. As God's people, we need to promote justice and fight injustice wherever we find it. You can't do everything, but you can do something.

GOD IS TICKED OFF BY SPIRITUAL COMPLACENCY

At the heart of complacency is pride. Complacency is believing that we're doing just fine. We think we have enough of God and don't need any more. This was the heart of Israel's complacency, and it ticked God off. The people were proud of the fact that God was with them. They thought they could get by with their false teaching and injustice, and that God would turn a deaf ear. It was a grave miscalculation:

> Yet all of you claim you are depending on the LORD. "No harm can come to us," you say, "for the LORD is here among us."
> So because of you, Mount Zion will be plowed like an open field; Jerusalem will be reduced to rubble! (Micah 3:11–12)

How to Please God

Very often people accuse God of being a cosmic kill-joy. They can't see why anyone would want to become a Christian, because God forbids

Christians to have fun. All the Bible is good for is telling us what's wrong with us. Christianity is nothing but a set of rules and regulations. How come God never tells us that we're doing a good job?

Yeah, it would be great if God were some kind of almighty motivational speaker that pumped us up at the beginning of every day with a rousing speech and a set of tapes, but that's not His style. God won't pat us on the back like a football coach and tell us what we're doing right, but He will tell us how to do what's right. God wants us to obey Him, because He knows us like nobody else, and He knows what's good for us. And when we do what God wants us to do, we are living the kind of abundant life that only a child of God can live.

So how do we please God? Is it merely avoiding the things that tick Him off? Well, that's a good place to start, but we also have to be proactive. We have to love God with all our souls, hearts, minds, and strength—in other words, with every part of our beings.

The people of Israel heard Micah's warnings, and they decided to change. They wanted to know how to please God and how to love Him more. They asked the prophet, "What can we bring to the LORD to make up for what we've done?" (6:6). They wanted to know if God required more offerings, more gifts, and more sacrifices. But God doesn't need our works. He doesn't want our sacrifices. David wrote:

> You would not be pleased with sacrifices, or I would bring them. If I brought you a burnt offering, you would not accept it. (Psalm 51:16)

So what does God want? David answers his own question:

> The sacrifice you want is a broken spirit. A broken and repentant heart, O God, you will not despise. (Psalm 51:17)

Micah answered the people in exactly the same way. God didn't need their sacrifices. What He wanted was a willing and obedient heart.

> No, O people, the LORD has already told you what is good, and this is what he requires: to do what is right, to love mercy, and to walk humbly with your God. (6:8)

This is one of the most famous verses in all of the Old Testament, and for a good reason. Here in just a few words God outlines the way to please him. These are words to live by.

Do What Is Right

Knowing what is right is easier than we think, because God has built a sense of right and wrong into each of us (Romans 2:15). What's tough is *doing* what is right. Yet that's exactly what God expects us to do. If we do the right thing, God is pleased. If we know what we should do, and we don't do it, God is not pleased (James 4:17).

Doing what is right doesn't stop with making right decisions where our own behavior is concerned. We also have to treat other people right. We must act justly in all situations.

Love Mercy

The definition of mercy is: not giving someone what he or she deserves. That's what God does for us every single day of our lives. "By his mercies we have been kept from complete destruction," wrote Jeremiah. "Great is his faithfulness; his mercies begin afresh each day" (Lamentations 3:22–23). That's the attitude God wants us to have toward each other. When we feel like destroying someone with a biting comment or a hateful thought, God expects us to have mercy. When we feel morally superior to someone, God expects us to have mercy.

Loving mercy means more than acting in a merciful way. James Boice writes: "We are to love it in others, and we are to love it as God develops that characteristic in ourselves."

Walk Humbly with Your God

Have you ever heard someone talk about "the Christian walk"? Or has anyone asked you if you were "walking with the Lord"? Sometimes we use ordinary words to describe our extraordinary relationships with God, and we wonder if the words are appropriate. In the case of your life with God, the word *walk* is a great description.

When you walk with someone you love, you don't walk ahead or behind; you walk side by side. That's what God wants for us. He wants us to walk with Him in humility. Our natural inclination is to walk in pride, but that only separates us from God. When we walk humbly, we recognize that God is the source of our strength, our wisdom, and our very lives.

You Can Make a Difference

Micah was only one person, yet his perseverance and the power of his message persuaded King Hezekiah to lead the people in repentance. King Hezekiah was only one person, yet his actions secured peace and God's blessing for an entire nation. How about you?

The Bible makes it clear that God is looking for people who will do what He requires so that through Him they can make a difference: "The eyes of the LORD search the whole earth in order to strengthen those whose hearts are fully committed to him" (2 Chronicles 16:9).

Where Is Another God Like You?

The book of Micah ends with a beautiful song of praise to God (7:18–20). Having reflected on God's mercy and deliverance, and no doubt remembering God's promise to send "the source of our peace" (5:5), Micah made it clear that there is none like God. He is the one who

- pardons our sins
- cannot stay angry with us
- delights in showing us mercy
- has compassion on us
- tramples our sins and throws them into the depths of the ocean
- shows us His faithfulness
- loves us with an everlasting love

This is a God we can trust to get us through any problem and to help us deal with any injustice. God has told us what He requires of us. All we have to do is follow His lead.

NOW I'M SORRY. NOW I'M NOT.

As humans, we are rather dense. So in describing the nature of our spiritual relationship with Him, God used an analogy we could all understand: *family*. God is our heavenly *Father;* we are His *children;* those who believe in God are *brothers and sisters* in the faith. We are the *family of God*.

Sometimes, it is a dysfunctional family. But that is never the fault of the Father. It is always due to the immaturity or rebellion of the children.

Do you ever wonder how God feels when we, as His spiritual children, are guilty of infantile behavior? It is not hard to imagine, at least not for those of us who are parents and have had our patience tested by a strong-willed child. This is why the "family" analogy works so well in teaching us principles of God's character. From your experiences as a human parent dealing with your child, you get a glimpse into how our Heavenly Father might see you.

Remember when your child was six months old and wailing for a bottle of milk? You were in the process of getting it ready. The bottle was heating in the microwave. It was only going to take twenty more seconds, yet the howling didn't subside. Out of frustration you were about ready to scream, "Oh, pipe down, you little piglet! Can't you see that I'm getting exactly what you need? Can't you just trust me and wait a few more seconds?" (OK, maybe a mom doesn't call her baby a "piglet." Maybe that's just a dad thing.)

Imagine, then, how patient God must be. Like screeching infants, we go crying to Him whenever we don't get what we want. So we whine about it to God, and we begin to doubt His provision. Throughout it all, however, God knows exactly what we need, and He is working in the details of our lives to make it happen. He endures our moaning and complaining. Maybe He thinks to Himself, "Can't you just trust me and wait a few more seconds," but He never loses His cool—and He never resorts to calling us "piglet."

Such theological insights aren't limited to experiences with infants and toddlers. Just as teenagers seek to assert their independence from parental control, we often rebel from God's spiritual authority. Many parents have experienced the pain of an adult child who rejects the family's values and gets involved in a lifestyle that is abhorrent to the parents. God also knows this pain. We have put Him through it far too many times, and you have to. But the story of the Prodigal Son illustrates God's forgiving nature and the fact that He is anxious to be reconciled with us, even when we have turned our backs on Him.

The parable of the Prodigal Son had a happy ending (except for the older brother who sulked and for the fatted calf that was roasted). And real-life reconciliations of this type are worthy of celebration, but the family relationship doesn't always stay happy. In real life, the wayward child who has repented may later return to the same inappropriate conduct. And what if that cycle of offense/remorse/offense was repeated time after time? Would it make you mad if your teenager did that to you? Well, not surprisingly, it makes God mad when we do it to Him.

God Gets Ticked off When We Repent of Sin and Later Return to It

That statement brings us to the prophet Nahum. His message to the people of Nineveh makes it clear that God is sorely displeased when we revoke our repentance by returning to our evil ways. You might never have pictured God in the way that Nahum describes Him, and we are sure that you won't ever want to, but it is an aspect of God's character that you need to know.

Don't Let the Name Fool You. There's Nothing Ho-hum about Nahum

The Old Testament book of Nahum is rather obscure. Although that can be said about most of the Minor Prophets, it is particularly true of Nahum. Admit it. When was the last time you started your day off by reading a passage from Nahum? Or heard a sermon preached from that text? We suspect that Nahum is perhaps the least popular of the Minor Prophets for two major reasons: First, it's not the most entertaining book you'll ever read, and besides that, it's difficult to understand without a historical perspective. Second, Nahum presents a picture of God that we really don't want to see.

The book of Nahum describes the terrible wrath of God. He is portrayed as a Divine Warrior who obliterates those who incur His wrath. Most of us don't want to be reminded of that aspect of God's character. We are partial to His attributes like love and forgiveness. But God is not one-dimensional. There is a flip side to love and forgiveness: He is also a God of justice and holy anger. We can try to ignore the less-appealing aspects of God's nature, but that won't make them go away. We can try to reinvent Him into the kind of God we want Him to be, but that doesn't change Him. We can even ignore the biblical teaching of God's nature and pretend that He is the kind of God we *feel* in our gut that He ought to be; but our gastrointestinal theology doesn't change who God really is. As much as we may want to avoid being confronted by a God of terrible wrath, this characteristic is an aspect of His nature. The book of Nahum makes that painfully clear.

Who Was Nahum?

The prophet Nahum was an obscure little guy. He isn't mentioned anywhere else in the Bible except in the book that bears his name. We are told that he hailed from the town of Elkosh, but Bible scholars haven't been able to determine the location of that town. (It's kind of like how we feel being from Fresno.) Some believe that Elkosh was in the northern part of Israel, perhaps around Galilee, but Nahum's message appears to be intended to give comfort to the residents in the southern region of Judah.

Nahum popped onto the scene sometime in the mid- to early seventh century B.C. He makes a reference to the conquest of Thebes (a historical event that occurred in 664 B.C.), and he predicts the destruction of Nineveh (another event that happened in 612 B.C.), so his message was delivered sometime between those two dates. The exact date is not important, but it must be realized that Nahum spoke at a time when Assyria dominated the entire Near East region.

Flashback

Assyria had always been a brutal and oppressive nation. But the residents in its capital city of Nineveh had experienced a spiritual repentance in 760 B.C. as a result of the preaching of Jonah. In a sincere display of remorse for their evil ways, the King of Assyria and the Ninevites called upon the name of the Lord and went through the whole sackcloth-and-ashes routine (but you already knew that from reading chapter 5). Within the span of one generation, however, the citizens of Nineveh returned to their evil ways. Their tenderhearted sorrow for sin had been replaced with an arrogant belief that they could live as decadently as they wanted. The Ninevites, and the entire nation of Assyria, abandoned any belief in God, and their remorse was long forgotten. By 722 B.C., Assyria invaded and captured the northern nation of Israel.

What Was Going On?

During the days of Nahum, the northern nation of Israel had been besieged and captured by Assyria. As was their usual practice, the Assyrians resettled the Jews from Israel to other regions, and other conquered peoples were brought into Israel. The southern nation of Judah was still in existence, but it was hanging by a thread. Judah was a vassal state, a slave to Assyria. Assyria oppressed Judah in every respect: economically, socially, politically, and religiously. There was a constant threat of imminent invasion and conquest.

The Jews in Judah had reason to live in fear. The Assyrians were notorious for their cruelty and violence. Their atrocities are legendary in history. Like all marauding nations, they ransacked and plundered every country they invaded. But the brutality of the Assyrians was particularly merciless and inhumane. Historians have documented their viciousness to include:

- impaling the corpses of their victims on poles that were placed around the wall of the vanquished city;
- cutting the lips off the faces of the people they captured;
- stacking the corpses like firewood and using them as fuel for bonfires; and
- impaling the jaw of a captured king with a knife, inserting a chain through his jaw, and then leading him around the city like a dog on a leash.

With this type of torture and sadistic cruelty, the Assyrians ravaged the various peoples of the ancient Near East for two hundred years. The residents of Judah and the capital of Jerusalem knew that this brand of inhumanity was their fate unless God intervened.

Nahum Brings a Mixed Message

Just when the Jews in Judah could feel the hot breath of the Assyrians, Nahum speaks up. His name can be translated to mean "comfort" or "compassion," and that was part of his message. But the rest of his message proclaimed doom and gloom. This bifurcated message was intended for two separate audiences, depending upon which side of the border they were on:

> FOR THE JEWS: God will show compassion on His people. As the Divine Warrior, He will protect them from the oppression of the Assyrians.

> FOR THE ASSYRIANS: God's wrath will be poured out upon the Assyrians as judgment for their atrocities. As the Divine Warrior, God will cause the destruction of Assyria and the obliteration of its capital city, Nineveh.

If you were a Jew in Judah listening to Nahum's message, you probably breathed a sigh of relief. If you were an Assyrian and heard Nahum's message, you might have wondered if your next breath would be your last.

Nahum Makes It Clear: Nineveh Ticked God Off!

The book of Nahum is only three chapters long. But lots of theology is crammed into its forty-seven verses. Nahum describes the wrath of God as it is directed against Nineveh (the representative seat of power for Assyria), but Nahum doesn't leave you thinking that God is unfair or irrational in the administration of His judgment. Interwoven with the verses describing God's fury are the reasons why Nineveh must suffer this righteous condemnation.

Nahum had some very insightful comments about God.

God gets jealous. In our culture, jealousy is not usually considered a virtue. We refer to the "green-eyed monster of jealousy." And don't forget the expression "Jealousy rearing its ugly head." So, you might find it interesting that Nahum describes God as being jealous:

> The LORD is a jealous God, filled with vengeance and wrath.
> (Nahum 1:2)

But there is a proper form of jealousy, too. For example, a husband or a wife should be jealous if a third person threatens the sanctity of their marriage. And parents should be jealously protective of anyone or anything that would harm their children. In the same way, God is jealous when people turn away from Him because He knows what is best for them, and any other alternative is destructive. God's jealousy does not involve petty envy; instead, it implies that God is worthy of absolute and exclusive devotion from all people. God's jealousy is not motivated by selfishness. Just the opposite. It arises from His commitment to righteousness and His concern for the object of His love.

God gets angry. Yes, God has patience with humanity, but His patience does not allow Him to tolerate sin.

> The LORD is slow to get angry, but his power is great, and he never lets the guilty go unpunished. (1:3)

God's anger is not uncontrollable and unpredictable. It doesn't flare up like your temper when you stub your toe or a driver cuts you off on the freeway. God's anger is always controlled and meted out fairly to those who deserve it. But once released, the power of God's anger is devastating.

> Who can survive his burning fury? His rage blazes forth like
> fire, and the mountains crumble to dust in his presence. . . .
> Why are you scheming against the LORD? He will destroy you
> with one blow; he won't need to strike twice! (1:6, 9)

God gets even. The patience of the Lord should not be presumed
upon or trifled with. He is a God of vengeance and retribution. Unlike humans, He has no thirst for revenge (which is simply a means
to gain power, and we all know that God doesn't need any more
power). God's wrath is a response to injustice and is administered in
an accurate assessment of what is right and wrong. His wrath is
always proportionate to the severity of the offense. In the case of
Nineveh, that meant complete annihilation.

> This is what the LORD says: "Even though the Assyrians have
> many allies, they will be destroyed and disappear. . . . And
> this is what the LORD says concerning the Assyrians in
> Nineveh: "You will have no more children to carry on your
> name. I will destroy all the idols in the temples of your gods.
> I am preparing a grave for you because you are despicable
> and don't deserve to live!" . . . All this because Nineveh, the
> beautiful and faithless city, mistress of deadly charms, enticed
> the nations with her beauty. She taught them all to worship
> her false gods, enchanting people everywhere. "No wonder I
> am your enemy!" declares the LORD Almighty. (1:12, 14;
> 3:4–5)

The Rest of the Story

We can't leave the prophecy of Nahum without telling you what
eventually happened. Within a decade or two of Nahum's message,
the unthinkable happened. The mighty Assyrian nation began to
crumble. God used the Babylonian empire, with their allies from
Median, to accomplish the capture and annihilation of Nineveh in
612 B.C. Within the next three years, the entire Assyrian nation was
conquered and under the dominion of the Babylonians. The

Babylonian armies destroyed Nineveh in precisely the manner that Nahum had prophesied. For many centuries, there was not even a trace of any city on the spot where archaeologists believed that Nineveh existed. Recent excavations, however, have unearthed some rubble and broken fragments that verify the former existence of Nineveh on that site.

Nahum's God Is Our God

The book of Nahum brings some of us to the shocking realization that God can get very angry, and the repercussions are not pretty. But you don't have to take our word for it. Just ask anyone from Nineveh. (Oops, you can't ask them because they were obliterated. Guess that proves our point.)

Nahum's God of wrath from the Old Testament didn't have a personality makeover during the time period covered by that blank page between the Old and New Testaments. He is the same God. So the characteristics revealed in the book of Nahum must be factored in to your concept of who God is and what He requires of us.

God Is Not Schizophrenic; He's Multifaceted

God can't tolerate sin. It would be against His holy nature. Consequently, He insists that sin be punished. Always.

"Wait a minute," some may say, "what about the *love* of God?" Well, it is true that God is love. But that isn't all that He is. He is also holy. When you combine His holiness with other characteristics such as righteousness and justice, you discover that not only can He not tolerate sin, but He must also impose punishment for it. You can't pick and choose the attributes of God that you like and assemble Him in the fashion you prefer. God is not a spiritual Mr. Potato Head.

Like it or not (and most of us don't), it is the nature of our God to impose a corrective process on unrepentant rebellious conduct. Like it or not (and all of us don't), that process includes three steps:

Actual. It really happens. Oh, you might not be the victim of an attack by a marauding gang of Assyrians, but God will make something happen. He can work in the details of your life (through other people or your circumstances) to bring about the corrective measures that He intends. The consequences of your actions may not be immediate, but there will be consequences.

Active. Don't think that you have escaped God's notice if you manage to live in defiance of His principles without any divine catastrophic retribution. Remember that God is slow to anger. God is not oblivious to what you're doing. He may be giving you a chance to repent (just like Nineveh . . . the first time). Be assured that He is aware and active in the oversight of your life. Unless you turn away from your immoral activities, God may bring corrective measures into your life (just like Nineveh . . . the second time).

Absolute. Don't cling to the desperate hope that God's plan might malfunction at the last minute. It is going to happen whether you like it or not. He won't be accepting any of your flimsy excuses.

God Knows Which Way the Wind Is Blowing

A less astute reader might miss the irony, but we are sure you caught it. The citizens of Nineveh were spared from annihilation when they repented of their sin in response to the preaching of Jonah. About 150 years later, God caused their destruction for the same kind of conduct. Is there an inconsistency here? Was God in a good disposition during the time of Jonah but irritable during the time of Nahum? Was it simply a divine mood swing?

When you contrast the stories of Jonah and Nahum, there was a big difference in the results. But God wasn't the one that changed. Nineveh was. When Nineveh was repentant, God spared the city and withheld His judgment. But when Nineveh recanted its remorse and resumed it decadence, arrogance, and cruelty, then God followed through with His judgment.

We both hail from the agriculture region of California's Central Valley. (When you are from farm country, you use words like "hail from" instead of simply saying "live in.") A weather vane on the top of a barn is a common site. Some people could look at a weather vane and say that it changes all of the time. It may be pointing to the north, but then quickly alter and point to the west. Moments later it could shift to the south or east. Does that mean that the weather vane is unreliable? No, on the contrary, a weather vane is entirely reliable because is operates according to an unchangeable principle: It *always* points to the direction from which the wind is blowing. Always. In that sense, the weather vane is unchangeable.

We need to view God in that same context. He will always respond favorably to a person who is truly repentant. And He will always respond with some sort of judgment or correction when a person is living in outright rebellion.

God Loves You Enough to Discipline You

Don't think that you can live in defiance to God's principles yet escape His discipline just because you are a Christian. As part of God's family, your sins are forgiven; that ensures you won't suffer eternal obliteration. Yet He may still bring discipline into the events of your life. As part of His family, you are loved and cherished by God. He doesn't want you harmed, even by your own self-damaging conduct. He may do whatever it takes to rescue you from you.

This principle is clearly illustrated in the saga of the children of Israel. Although they were God's "chosen people," God brought severe events into their lives in order to turn their wayward hearts back to Him. But this principle is not limited to the Old Testament. The writer of the book of Hebrews explained it this way:

> As you endure this divine discipline, remember that God is treating you as his own children. Whoever heard of a child who was never disciplined? If God doesn't discipline you as he does all of his children, it means that you are illegitimate and are not really his children after all. Since we respect our earthly fathers who disciplined us, should we not all the more cheerfully submit to the discipline of our heavenly Father and live forever?
>
> For our earthly fathers disciplined us for a few years, doing the best they knew how. But God's discipline is always right and good for us because it means we will share in his holiness. No discipline is enjoyable while it is happening—it is painful! But afterward there will be a quiet harvest of right living for those who are trained in this way. (Hebrews 12:7–11)

The love of God is inseparable from the discipline of God because His discipline is a manifestation of His love.

We've Ticked God off (and Continue to Do So)

The citizens of Nineveh offended God and incurred His wrath when they disobeyed Him by returning to the very same immoral lifestyle of which they had earlier repented. God detested this in-your-face behavior. To have completely abandoned any sense of remorse and reverted to the same conduct was nothing short of outright insolence and rebellion against God. It is completely understandable that God was ticked off at such defiance.

Because God doesn't change, the message of Nahum is as applicable now as it was in the seventh century B.C. That means it's time to get personal. We might think that we are better than the Ninevites, but we are not. Going to church, reading the Bible, financially supporting a missionary or two, and reciting the prayer of Jabez doesn't erase this fundamental fact:

WE TICK GOD OFF EVERY TIME WE RETURN TO THE SIN THAT WE PREVIOUSLY CONFESSED

This should be a sobering and saddening thought for each of us. When we intentionally sin *again*, we are engaged in an act of outright defiance and rebellion against God. Our repeated sin is no trivial matter. It doesn't matter whether that conduct involves sexual sin, substance abuse, anger, materialism, idolatry, selfishness, gossip, or spiritual arrogance. Every volitional act on our part that knowingly takes us back into sin is an egregious affront to God.

The essence of repentance is to turn from your sin and walk in the other direction. Sincere remorse and true sorrow over sin imply the recognition that it is wrong and indicate the desire to refrain from it ever again. Assuming that we are truly repentant when we sin, why do we so easily return to it? Perhaps we don't realize how offensive our sin is to God. Maybe we are taking His ever-ready forgiveness for granted.

Until we get to heaven we will never fully understand the magnitude of God's grace. Right now, as earth dwellers, we have just a hint of it. Even so, that is no excuse for abusing it. Our appreciation for the great gift of God's grace should cause us to sin less, not more. As the apostle Paul said:

> Well then, should we keep on sinning so that God can show us more and more kindness and forgiveness? Of course not! (Romans 6:1)

What We Can Do about It

What is the solution to the repetitive sin problem that entangles us so frequently? Death is one answer, but that seems a bit drastic. A less fatal alternative, but one more difficult to achieve, would be to pursue personal holiness. Of course, that is easier said than done, but it is what our response to God should be in the first place.

No one will dispute that the pursuit for personal holiness involves a struggle. Most of us are engaged in the battle on a daily basis. But often we don't reflect on the nature of the struggle.

- It is not a conflict of logic or reason. We all know the benefits of following God's precepts and the damage caused by sin.
- It is not an intellectual battle. We usually know what is right and what is wrong. Whenever we struggle with repetitive sin, there is a distinct line that separates the choices.
- It is not a fight between our loyalties. We'll take God over Satan every time.

> Repentance consists of the heart being broken from sin. Some often repent, yet never reform; they resemble a man traveling in a dangerous path, who frequently starts and stops, but never turns back.
>
> —Bonnell Thornton

The real struggle for personal holiness involves *motivation*. Oftentimes we are more motivated by the pleasure of sin, and that is what draws us back into the quagmire. We stay trapped in repetitive sin not because the Holy Spirit within us is weak, but because we are relying on the wrong motivation for personal holiness.

If you refrain from sin because you are worried about jeopardizing God's love for you, then your motivation will frequently be insufficient to keep you from sinning. Likewise, your motivation is faulty if you are trying to impress God with how good you are. Either way, your attempts are motivated out of self-interest and doomed for failure. Your self-interest in securing God's favor almost always loses out to your self-satisfying desire for the pleasure of sin.

More significantly, such an attitude obscures your understanding of God's grace. You are trying to secure God's love by what *you* do (or don't do). Such an attitude is completely contrary to the forgiveness that God offers. The wonderful, overriding principle of God's grace assures us that there is nothing we can do that would make God love us less; likewise, there is nothing we can do that would make God love us more. God's love is unconditional.

The best motivation for personal holiness is gratitude for God's grace. As we begin to grow in our understanding of God, then our love for Him increases. As our love for God grows, our motivation for personal holiness increases. Personal holiness is less of a struggle only when we begin to love God as a natural response to the love He has first shown toward us (see 1 John 4:19).

The apostle Paul understood that repetitive sin comes much more naturally than personal holiness.

> I don't understand myself at all, for I really want to do what is right, but I don't do it. Instead, I do the very thing I hate. I know perfectly well that what I am doing is wrong. . . . But I can't help myself. . . . No matter which way I turn, I can't make myself do right. I want to, but I can't. When I want to do good, I don't. And when I try not to do wrong, I do it anyway. (Romans 7:15–19)

But Paul also realized that a greater appreciation of God's love would produce a change in our behavior:

And so, dear brothers and sisters, I plead with you to give your bodies to God. Let them be a living and holy sacrifice— the kind he will accept. When you think of what he has done for you, is this too much to ask? (Romans 12:1)

Personal holiness involves spiritual discipline over your thoughts (Philippians 4:8) and your actions (1 Corinthians 9:12), and it begins with the knowledge of God. As you know more of Him, you will love Him more. As your love for God increases, your desire to return to sin will decrease. That's why Paul prayed more about increasing in the knowledge of God than about refraining from sin.

When I think of the wisdom and scope of God's plan, I fall to my knees and pray to the Father, the Creator of everything in heaven and on earth. I pray that from his glorious, unlimited resources he will give you mighty inner strength through his Holy Spirit. And I pray that Christ will be more and more at home in your hearts as you trust in him. May your roots go down deep into the soil of God's marvelous love. And may you have the power to understand, as all God's people should, how wide, how long, how high, and how deep his love really is. May you experience the love of Christ, though it is so great you will never fully understand it. Then you will be filled with the fullness of life and power that comes from God. (Ephesians 3:14–19)

GOD AND EVIL

It was a totally unexpected attack that shocked people for its violence and cruelty. Nothing like it had ever been experienced before. This was a new kind of threat and power that surprised everyone by infiltrating the very culture it intended to conquer.

The terrorists came from distant Middle Eastern places, like a wind from the desert. They mocked those in authority and slipped through the national defenses. Their attack came like an eagle from the air, and they swooped down to pounce on their prey. The results were devastating.

The nation mourned its victims while the experts looked for answers. Why did this violence happen? How can such evil exist in the world? Would justice be done? Many looked to God; some for comfort, and others to ask, "Where was God in all of this?" Some spiritual leaders boldly proclaimed that God had caused the attack as a punishment for sin, while others said God had nothing to do with it.

• • •

If this historical account sounds familiar, it should, but it's not what you think. This may seem like a news account of the events of September 11, 2001. In fact, it's a paraphrase of the first chapter of Habakkuk, a Minor Prophet who delivered his message between the fall of Nineveh in 612 B.C. and the destruction of Jerusalem in 586 B.C. The nation under attack was Judah, and the "new power" was the Babylonians, who were unusually cruel and ruthless. They were proud of their unconventional warfare tactics, which they used to conquer the people of God and destroy the mighty city of Jerusalem.

A Modern-Day Prophet

This piece of history and the nations and people involved may be different from our own, but the issues are remarkably similar. Habakkuk was the prophet sent by God to speak to the people of Judah, who were enjoying prosperity in a nation filled with wickedness and violence. Though their nation had been founded on God's law, He was being ignored. Habakkuk found himself "surrounded by people who love to argue and fight" (1:3). As he observed the court systems, Habakkuk concluded:

> The law has become paralyzed and useless, and there is no justice given in the courts. The wicked far outnumber the righteous, and justice is perverted with bribes and trickery. (1:4)

Habakkuk would feel right at home in our society, wouldn't he? Plop the wise prophet in front of the television for a day, let him watch a few episodes of the *Jerry Springer* show and Court TV, and he would see plenty of arguing and fighting. Drop the man of God into the middle of South Central or East L. A. on any given night, where gang-related murders are up 143 percent, and he would see destruction and violence wherever he looked.

Seeing these images of violence, destruction, and injustice in Jerusalem in 600 B.C. prompted Habakkuk to ask God some hard-hitting questions in verses 2 and 3.

- "How long, O LORD, must I call for help?"
- "'Violence!' I cry, but you do not come to save."
- "Must I forever see this sin and misery all around me?"

Seeing similar images in our cities twenty-six hundred years later should prompt us to ask the same questions of God.

God Answers Habakkuk

Of course, when we ask God direct questions, we need to be prepared for direct answers. And in this case, they weren't the kind of answers the prophet was expecting (there's another lesson for us).

Go Ahead and Ask God

Habakkuk has been called the doubting Thomas of the Old Testament. He wasn't afraid to ask God the tough questions that really bothered him, and God wasn't offended by his honesty. John Phillips wrote: "We can learn a valuable lesson from Habakkuk, for this man, when faced with a seemingly unsolvable problem, took it to God, instead of abandoning his faith as some would do."[1] God doesn't mind our questions or our doubts. He's big enough to handle them and gracious enough to answer.

Basically God told Habakkuk to stand back and watch what He would do. He wasn't going to save the people. On the contrary, he was going to bring even more destruction and violence. God promised to raise up the Babylonians to conquer Judah and carry the people into captivity. There was one simple reason for this:

GOD IS TICKED OFF WHEN WE TRUST OURSELVES INSTEAD OF TRUSTING HIM

Habakkuk accepted God's response, but he didn't completely understand it. Why would God use evil and evil people to punish his own people? Habakkuk's words reflect the anguish in his heart:

> O LORD my God, my Holy One, you who are eternal—is your plan in all of this to wipe us out? Surely not! (1:12)

That sure sounds familiar! We would be less than honest if we didn't ask God a question like that in response to a horrible calamity, whether it's a terrorist attack that kills thousands or a devastating earthquake that takes ten thousand lives. Then there's the awful, repulsive thought that God may actually be using these killers to punish his people. It occurred to Habakkuk, so he asked God. And even in the process of asking, he tried to reconcile his belief in a just God with what he perceived to be unjust actions.

O L ORD our Rock, you have decreed the rise of these Babylonians to punish and correct us for our terrible sins. You are perfectly just in this. But will you, who cannot allow sin in any form, stand idly by while they swallow us up? Should you be silent while the wicked destroy people who are more righteous than they? (1:12–13)

Have you ever felt this kind of emotional conflict when you observe the atrocities that go on in our world? We sure have. How can we reconcile our belief in a just and righteous and good God, who has our best interests in mind at all times, with the horrible things God allows to happen?

That's not an easy question to ask, and we can take comfort in the fact that it wasn't easy for this messenger of God either. Habakkuk continued to wrestle with the issue and to vent his frustrations. Speaking on behalf of his people—God's people—he cried out to God, "We're like fish in a barrel! We're sitting ducks. Our enemies are going to catch us and string us up, and they're going to rejoice over their success as they give praise to their gods. How long are you going to let these evil people get away with this?"

Questions for the Ages

The book of Habakkuk was written twenty-six hundred years ago by a Jewish prophet, but a social critic could have just as easily published it today. The questions concerning God and the problem of evil are as relevant to us as they were to Judah, mainly because they concern some of the huge issues that confront us every single day. These are the questions that Christians and skeptics alike ask about God because they go to the very foundation of who God is. They are questions about evil and pain and suffering, and why a God of goodness and love would allow all of it to happen.

We want to explore the questions Habakkuk asks, as well as some of the related issues. It's not our purpose to give you all of the answers (mainly because we can't), but we do want to help you to think through what all of this means and how it affects your life. Whether or not you have a personal relationship with God, you have wrestled with these questions.

Arguing about God Proves He Exists

Some people try to solve the problem of evil this way: If evil exists, then God cannot exist, because God is good, and He wouldn't allow evil. Therefore, since evil exists, God can't exist. That conclusion may sound plausible, but it is a moral impossibility. If God does not exist, then our conscience about good and evil does not exist either. Any moral outrage about what we perceive to be wrong is simply a personal, subjective feeling. But that's not the way it is. When something is morally wrong, there is a collective belief that it is wrong. This points to a Creator, who built this sense of morality into His created beings (Romans 2:14–15). Without God as conscience giver, we couldn't tell right from wrong or good from bad.

Why Is There Evil and Why Doesn't God Stop It?

The question of evil goes to the heart of pain and suffering, and this includes the pain and suffering inflicted by nature and disease (*physical* evil), and the pain and suffering inflicted by other human beings (*moral* evil). It's all part of the same problem. We dealt with physical evil (mostly natural disasters) in chapter 2, so we're going to focus on moral evil in this chapter. C. S. Lewis wrote that this kind of evil "accounts for four-fifths of the sufferings of men."[2]

What Is Evil?

Theologians have wrestled with the problem of God and evil co-existing in the same universe for centuries, so we aren't going to come up with anything new here. However, there are some basic things we can build on. First, we need to look at the characteristics of both terms.

God is the one true self-existent God of the Bible and of history. God is the *creator* of the heavens and the earth (Genesis 1:1); He is *eternal* (Psalm 90:2) and *infinite* (Revelation 1:8); He is *holy* (Isaiah 6:3); God *doesn't change* (Malachi 3:6), and He is completely *just* (Deuteronomy 32:4); God is *all-powerful* (Revelation 19:6), *all-knowing*

(Psalm 139:1–4), and He is *everywhere at once* (Psalm 139:7–12); and God is *love* (1 John 4:7–9).

Evil is the consequence of sin, which is anything that is contrary to God, His character, and His expressed will. The word *sin* literally means, "to miss the mark." Sin is anything that misses the mark of "God's glorious standard" (Romans 3:23). The Bible says that every single person is a sinner, due to the original sin of Adam (Romans 5:12). Therefore we are all inclined to sin and do evil because we are all sinners. Not a very pleasant thought, but it's the reality of the human condition.

Is God Responsible for Evil?

Since God created everything, isn't He also the author of evil? That whole thing in the garden with the apple and the snake and temptation was just a setup, right? Didn't God set a trap for humanity so we would sin? And if that's the case, wouldn't that make God—and not us—responsible for our sin?

Not in the least. Remember, God is holy and God is good. It is impossible for Him to do evil, therefore, He can't create evil. But He did open the door for evil to exist when He created human beings. You see, God could have made us as robots, programmed to love Him unconditionally, but He didn't want it that way. God created us as morally perfect beings with the ability to choose to love Him or not (after all, what good is *forced* love?).

Here's where God opened the door: By creating us with the freedom to choose to love Him or not, He allowed for the possibility of sin, which is simply choosing what we want over what God wants. It's putting ourselves in the place of God. C. S. Lewis wrote:

> Christianity asserts that God is good; that He made all things good and for the sake of their goodness; that one of the good things He made, namely, the free will of rational creatures, by its very nature included the possibility of evil; and that creatures, availing themselves of this possibility, have become evil.[3]

Don't be confused by people who say that a loving God could never permit evil. It's precisely because God loves us and wants us to freely love him back that evil exists. Theologian Dr. Norman Geisler wrote: "God created the *fact* of freedom, but we perform the *acts* of freedom. . . . Imperfection came through the abuse of our moral perfection as free creatures."[4]

So Why Doesn't God Destroy Evil?

This is really quite simple: Evil cannot be destroyed without destroying freedom. Another way to look at it is this: In order to destroy evil, God would have to destroy our freedom, which in itself would be evil, and God just can't do that.

Dr. Geisler advises that we speak about evil being *defeated,* not destroyed. God can do this, and He will, because He is all-good and all-powerful. Just because evil is not yet defeated doesn't mean that God won't defeat it someday. That day is coming. Of that we can be sure.

Why Is There So Much Evil?

You could also ask, "Why is there so much pain and suffering?" This is a reasonable question when asked from our perspective, but try looking at it from God's point of view. He created a perfect world with morally perfect human beings made in His perfect image. By our free choice, we contaminated His world with sin and evil on every level. By all rights, God should wipe us all out and start over. In fact, He almost did. God brought about a flood to wipe the human race off the face of the earth (Genesis 6:6–7), yet He had mercy and spared Noah and his family. God wanted to destroy Nineveh, but when God saw that the king and the citizens were willing to stop their evil ways, "He had mercy on them and didn't carry out the destruction he had threatened" (Jonah 3:10).

With all that the human race is capable of doing, perhaps the question should not be, Why do we suffer so much? but rather, Why don't we suffer more? We deserve the world we live in—a world full of evil and pain and suffering—but it could be worse. God could allow even more evil to exist, up to our very destruction by our own hands. But God loves us too much to allow it. The prophet Jeremiah was a contemporary of Habakkuk. He wrote:

> The unfailing love of the LORD never ends! By his mercies we have been kept from complete destruction. Great is his faithfulness; his mercies begin afresh each day. (Lamentations 3:22–23)

In his excellent book *Where Is God When It Hurts?* Philip Yancey wrote: "That this world spoiled by evil and suffering still exists is an example of God's mercy, not his cruelty."[5]

Does God Use Evil?

This is the right question to ask. What isn't right to ask is, Does God *cause* evil? God is incapable of causing evil, because He is completely holy and good. But it is proper to ask if He *uses* evil, along with pain and suffering. And the answer has to be yes.

If you've read some of the more popular stories in the Old Testament, you know that God often used evil, pain, and suffering to accomplish His purposes.

His brothers sold Joseph into slavery because they were jealous of him (make that *really* jealous). God directed his life and his circumstances to place him into a place of prominence in the nation of Egypt, where he was able to rescue his family and the Jewish nation from starvation. God used the evil deeds of Joseph's brothers to bring about a good result (Genesis 50:20).

Job was a blameless man of complete integrity who feared God and stayed away from evil (Job 1:1). Yet God allowed Satan to test Job in the most severe way possible, short of taking his life. The book of Job is not so much about suffering (although there's plenty of it) as it is about faith. Job's suffering strengthened his faith in God as the living Redeemer. "After my body has decayed, yet in my body I will see God!" he wrote (Job 19:26).

The Minor Prophets, including the Book of Habakkuk, are full of examples of God using evil: "Watch and be astounded at what I will do!" said God (Habakkuk 1:5). Clearly, God used the evil Babylonian empire.

But why? What's the purpose in God using evil? Well, sometimes God used evil to bring about a greater good (Joseph). Sometimes he used evil to develop greater faith (Job). And sometimes God used evil to punish sin (Habakkuk). But nowhere does the Bible tell us that God caused the pain and suffering or that He enjoyed it. As we pointed out earlier in this book, God simply used the evil that was already there—in the hearts of people, in the will of nations, even in the mind of Satan—to bring about a positive result.

Philip Yancey questions whether God uses pain of any kind to punish us. He argues in *Where Is God When It Hurts?* that the "'rules' governing God's contract relationship with the Israelites expressed a unique relationship that we cannot, nor should we expect to, emulate." He suggests, "We would do better to look at other biblical models,"[6] which is exactly what he does. Specifically, Yancey looks to the example of Jesus (always a good idea, by the way).

Jesus was nothing less than God in human form. When Jesus was born in the flesh, God entered human history. He became one of us. That incredible act of love and sacrifice changed the way God relates to us, and it changed the way God uses pain and suffering in our lives.

Jesus Teaches about Evil

There is a story in Luke 13 in which Jesus was informed about two separate but equally tragic events. One event involved Pilate, the Roman procurator of Judea who would later preside over the trial of Jesus. Evidently Pilate murdered some people from Galilee who were "sacrificing at the Temple in Jerusalem" (v. 1). The other event concerned a construction accident in Jerusalem that killed eighteen men. One was a moral evil and the other a physical evil.

Jesus used these two events to make a profound statement about God and evil. First, he posed the question that was on everyone's mind: "'Do you think those Galileans were worse sinners than other people from Galilee?' he asked. 'Is that why they suffered?'" (v. 2). And what of the eighteen men who died in the construction accident? "Were they the worst sinners in Jerusalem?" Jesus inquired (v. 4).

His answer to both questions was, "Not at all!" Then Jesus turned the tables on those who had not suffered, which was basically everyone else. "Unless you repent, you will also perish" (v. 5). Yancey observed:

He implies that we "bystanders" of catastrophe have as much to learn from the event, as do the victims. A tragedy should alert us to make ourselves ready in case we are the next victim of a falling tower, or an act of political terrorism. Catastrophe thus joins together victim and bystander in a call to repentance, by abruptly reminding us of the brevity of life.[7]

So it would seem that in our time, pain and suffering are warnings that all is not right with the world, and the only way for us to escape the finality of death (which comes to every person) is to call on the God who is able, willing, and ready to save us. To say that God allows certain tragedies to punish people for specific sins is counterproductive and contradictory to what Jesus taught.

Why Do Evil People Go Unpunished?

King David asked this very same question when he wrote:

> For I envied the proud when I saw them prosper despite their wickedness. (Psalm 73:3)

The truth is, it may seem as though evil people go unpunished and even prosper, but their time is coming. It's just that they aren't punished as rapidly as we would like. If terrorists strike us, we want to strike back immediately, and we expect God to do the same. But God doesn't operate on our timetable. He doesn't regard the passing of time as a measurement for action. For God, "a thousand years are as yesterday!" (Psalm 90:4).

Now that doesn't mean God is going to take a thousand years to punish the wicked. Habakkuk wondered when God was going to punish the Babylonians (1:17), and God responded:

> These things I plan won't happen right away. Slowly, steadily, surely, the time approaches when the vision will be fulfilled.
> If it seems slow, wait patiently, for it will surely take place. It will not be delayed. (2:3)

Remarkably, there is a very similar passage of Scripture in the New Testament that echoes these very same concepts. Only instead of focusing on a specific nation, the apostle Peter addresses everyone who needs to turn back to God.

> But you must not forget, dear friends, that a day is like a thousand years to the Lord, and a thousand years is like a day. The Lord isn't really being slow about his promise to return, as some people think. No, he is being patient for your sake. He does not want anyone to perish, so he is giving more time for everyone to repent. But the day of the Lord will come as unexpectedly as a thief. Then the heavens will pass away with a terrible noise, and everything in them will disappear in fire, and the earth and everything on it will be exposed to judgment. (2 Peter 3:8–10)

Someday God is going to deal with evil once and for all, and when that day comes His mercy will end. Whenever we get impatient with God's patience, we need to remember that He is waiting for the sake of the human race. God doesn't delight in pain and suffering. He longs for people to stop their evil ways and turn back to Him.

> Some other religions try to deny all pain, or to rise above it. Christianity starts, rather, with the assertion that suffering exists, and exists as proof of our fallen state.
>
> —Philip Yancey

Does Evil Have a Purpose?

We have already talked about some of the ways God uses evil, but these do not apply to every single person at any given moment. There is another much more personal aspect to pain and suffering, whether it comes from physical evil or moral evil, and it's this: God can use our pain and our suffering to get our attention. C. S. Lewis wrote that pain is "God's megaphone." It's the "terrible instrument" God uses to get our attention.

> Everyone has noticed how hard it is to turn our thoughts to God when everything is going well with us. We "have all we want" is a terrible saying when "all" does not include God.

We find God an interruption. As St. Augustine says some-where, "God wants to give us something, but cannot, because our hands are full—there's nowhere for Him to put it."[8]

How true! When we're on top of the world—even if we know God personally—we are less likely to think we need Him. But when we lose our jobs, get cancer, or experience the death of a friend, then we seek God. When kids kill kids in a high school, when terrorists murder thousands in a single day, we flood our churches and pray like we've never prayed before. When pain and suffering bring us to our knees, we stay there and cry out to God. So if evil and the pain and suffering it causes have a purpose, it's to bring us to God.

What Is God's Solution?

God has a solution to the age-old question of evil, and it's not what most people expect. If it were up to us to play God, we would prob-ably do one of two things. Either we would remove the suffering from the sufferer, or we would remove the sufferer from the suffering. That wasn't how God chose to deal with the wretched condition of this planet and its inhabitants. God did something totally unexpected and unimaginable. He entered *into* our world of pain and suffering, took on the body of a human, and lived His life among us.

Yes, someday God will remove us from the evil, defeat evil once and for all, and allow us to share in His glory. But first He had to suf-fer and experience our pain so that He could conquer the physical limitations of death for us. Is it too much for God to allow us to experience some pain and suffering of our own, so we can identify with what He did for us? The apostle Paul didn't think so:

> We are pressed on every side by troubles, but we are not crushed and broken. We are perplexed, but we don't give up and quit. We are hunted down, but God never abandons us. We get knocked down, but we get up again and keep going. Through suffering, these bodies of ours constantly share in the death of Jesus so that the life of Jesus may also be seen in our bodies. (2 Corinthians 4:8–10)

How Should We Respond?

We're almost done with this chapter, and we're just now getting back to the issue of what ticks God off. No, we didn't forget. We had to talk about evil and suffering first, and how we need to think about how we should respond. As always, God doesn't lock us in. He gives us the freedom of choice. In the context of God and evil, one choice ticks Him off, and the other choice pleases Him to no end.

Trust Yourself

This is the root of pride, and it ticks God off. It's right there in Habakkuk 2:4 where God said:

> Look at the proud! They trust in themselves, and their lives
> are crooked.

Where evil is concerned, pride is displayed in one of two ways. Either we think we can get through our troubles without God, or we use our pain and suffering as an excuse to turn our backs on Him. Either way, our pride represents our rebellion, and our pride ticks God off. God doesn't allow evil just so we can disregard it and move on. Pain and suffering aren't relevant only when it happens to us. When someone else hurts, God wants us to show compassion. When we hurt, He wants us to turn to Him.

Trust God

"Suffering is not good in itself," Lewis wrote. "What is good is— for the sufferer—his submission to the will of God and—for the spectators—the compassion aroused and the acts of mercy to which it leads."[9]

We may not always understand the nature of the evil that confronts us or the suffering that comes upon us. In fact, we may have a hard time understanding all of it most of the time. But that's no excuse for abandoning God. Even when we don't understand His ways, God wants us to trust Him. Even though we can't see the outcome, God wants us to trust Him. Even when God doesn't act according to our timetable, God wants us to trust Him. It's all about faith. God explains it clearly in the last part of the verse we talked about earlier:

> . . . but the righteous will live by their faith. (Habakkuk 2:4)

The Way of Faith

The Book of Habakkuk makes it clear that the challenge for every single person is to choose between the way of self, with its heartbreak and emptiness; or the way of faith, with its dependence on God. Only God is worthy of our faith, even when we don't understand everything he does. John Phillips wrote:

> Habakkuk, like so many of us, wanted to understand everything, but God showed him this could never be. Instead he must trust—trust God in the dark—for God is not going to give all the answers in this life.[10]

Faith is based on trust, and it builds perseverance. The writer of Hebrews defined faith this way: "It is the confident assurance that what we hope for is going to happen. It is the evidence of things we cannot yet see" (Hebrews 11:1). In this world filled with so much pain and suffering, we need to believe that God is going to deliver on what He promised.

> Do not throw away this confident trust in the Lord, no matter what happens. Remember the great reward it brings you! Patient endurance is what you need now, so you will continue to do God's will. Then you will receive all that he has promised.
> "For in just a little while,
>> the Coming One will come and not delay.
> And a righteous person will live by faith.
>> But I will have no pleasure in anyone who turns away."
> But we are not like those who turn their backs on God and seal their fate. We have faith that assures our salvation. (Hebrews 10:35–39)

9

GOD OR NO GOD?
DOES IT REALLY MAKE A DIFFERENCE?

in•dif•fer•ent: *adj.* (1) having or showing no interest, concern or feeling; (2) uninterested, apathetic, or unmoved; (3) detached; (4) lacking emotional involvement.

Indifference. We are all indifferent about one thing or another. Stan likes to follow the daily sports reports on ESPN; Bruce is indifferent to all of that. On the other hand, Stan is indifferent to the obituaries, but they are the first things Bruce reads in the newspaper each morning (he's not morbid; he's just a probate lawyer). But those are just two of our many idiosyncrasies. You've got your own personal list of things that fall into this category: things you don't *love*, but you don't *hate* them—you're just indifferent to them. Your personal list might include: the color taupe, accountants, any movie starring Eddie Murphy, or lima beans.

Many times, indifference doesn't matter. With certain things, however, your life can be adversely affected by your indifference. For example, you are headed for trouble if you are indifferent about your health, your job, your family, or your finances. And, whether you realize it or not, you're headed for trouble if you are indifferent about your relationship with God, because . . .

GOD IS TICKED OFF BY OUR SPIRITUAL INDIFFERENCE

When you are indifferent toward God, your spiritual sensitivities are dulled. Your moral consciousness gets calloused to the point at which you don't hear the conviction of the Holy Spirit. You become increasingly entrenched in sin, and you don't even realize it.

Allow us to demonstrate the effects of indifference toward God with this hypothetical illustration: Suppose you are a frog. If we dropped you into a pan of boiling water, you would immediately jump out of the pan. But suppose that we placed you into a pan of cool water. You'd be croaking in pure delight. And because you have the mentality of a tailless, leaping amphibian, you are indifferent to slight changes in the water temperature. So you stay in the pan of water while we crank up the heat on the stove. As the temperature rises, your indifference makes you oblivious to the impending danger. Before too long, you have been boiled to death, and we'll be dipping your legs in melted butter for dinner.

The analogy is obvious. However, the mental image of us chomping on your butter-drenched legs might be so repulsive that you are unable to make the metaphorical connection. Not to worry. We can give you another illustration of the danger of being dulled to God's conviction. Perhaps you'll like this illustration better. (It still involves water and you dying, but at least the water isn't boiling and we won't eat you at the end.)

Suppose you are a person. (You like this illustration better already, don't you?) You are sitting on your couch, dividing your attention between watching ESPN and reading the obituaries in the newspaper. A news bulletin interrupts the normal programming with a flash-flood alert. But you are indifferent to the weather. What difference does it make? Life always goes on. So, you ignore the televised warnings. And you ignore the evacuation warnings from the police officer driving through your neighborhood. And, a few hours later, as you slosh around in your living room, you ignore the offer for a ride from a rescue worker as he maneuvers his boat down the rushing torrent of water where your street used to be. You're still engrossed in those obituaries (the television exploded when water reached the electrical outlet) as you climb onto the roof of your home. You are even indifferent to the offer of rescue from a Red Cross helicopter. A couple of days later, everyone reads *your* obituary.

And so it is with each of us if we are indifferent to God. His attempts to deal directly in our lives go unnoticed by us because we are uninterested and detached from Him. Indifference may be the worst of all spiritual conditions. Think about it:

Spiritual indifference is worse than believing in a false religion. In that case, you would be on the wrong track, but at least you would be aware of the importance of the spiritual dimension in your life. If you were truly seeking after God, all it would take to get you straightened out is the truth. Because you are spiritually minded, you wouldn't be resistant to the truth; you would be anxious to hear it.

Spiritual indifference is worse than giving something other than God first place in your life. In this situation, you remain interested in God, but your priorities are mixed up. God is still in your life, but your focus is centered on something else. There is a good chance that your attention can be corrected. You can be convinced of the folly of your priorities. Your divided heart, already partially directed to God, can be challenged and encouraged toward complete loyalty to Him.

Spiritual indifference is worse than if you have simply fallen out of fellowship with God. This condition is commonly referred to as "back-sliding" (which is not an extreme sport, but rather, a spiritual condition). When those who aren't walking with God find themselves in troubled times, they are quick to remember the peace they had with God in the past. Their current problems and their sacred memories cause them to return to their first love.

But the chances of connecting with God aren't as likely if you suffer from spiritual indifference. It is a form of practical atheism. Oh, maybe you don't actually deny God's existence, but your apathy puts you in a place where His existence simply doesn't matter. You have detached yourself from all sensitivity to spiritual influences. This is what makes spiritual indifference the most hopeless condition of all.

> God said of His people at one time that they turned their backs on him but not their faces. Such people continue looking in one direction, but they are all headed in the opposite direction. The Bible calls them "stiff-necked," for obvious reasons!
> —Stuart Briscoe

It should come as no surprise then that God is ticked off when we are indifferent toward Him. The eternal destiny of our souls may be in grave danger. If we are already part of God's family, our apathetic attitude toward Him is an act of ungrateful rebellion, and we must be disciplined for our own benefit.

But you don't have to take our word as proof that God is upset by indifference toward Him. Just read the words of the prophet Zephaniah.

The Prophet in the Palace

Zephaniah was the last of the Minor Prophets to preach in Judah before its captivity. The Assyrian Empire was beginning to crumble, and Babylonia was the up-and-coming world power that dealt the death-blow with the annihilation of Nineveh in 612 B.C. Those same Babylonians eventually conquered Judah with the destruction of Jerusalem in 586 B.C. But wait! We're getting ahead of ourselves.

Most of the prophets were dirt-poor itinerant preachers. Not Zephaniah. He was the only prophet to be born into a stately lineage. He was a descendant (four generations removed) of Hezekiah, the former king of Judah. His regal heritage is mentioned in the very first verse of his book. We doubt that he cited his ancestry because he had a big ego. It is more likely that mention of King Hezekiah is made to take the reader back to the memory of the good times when Judah experienced God's blessings under a good king. And that is exactly what Hezekiah was: a good, although not perfect, king.

> Hezekiah trusted in the LORD, the God of Israel. There was never another king like him in the land of Judah, either before or after his time. He remained faithful to the LORD in everything, and he carefully obeyed all the commands the LORD had given Moses. So the LORD was with him, and Hezekiah was successful in everything he did. (2 Kings 18:5–7)

The mere mention of King Hezekiah would remind the people of Judah of the blessings they experienced from God under the reign of that godly king. While Hezekiah was king, God protected them each time the Assyrians attempted to invade Jerusalem. At the same time, however, the northern kingdom of Israel and the neighboring region of Samaria were suffering under the oppression of the Assyrians because of prior unfaithfulness to God. It was a perfect illustration of God's age-old principle of blessing those who obeyed Him and bringing discipline upon those who lived in rebellion against Him.

But reciting Zephaniah's ancestral heritage did more than just remind the people of God's blessings during the reign of King Hezekiah. It also reminded them of the trouble that befell them under the rule of the successive kings who rejected God's principles.

Although Hezekiah had a heart for God, that coronary condition wasn't inherited by his son, Manasseh. Manasseh might have been Judah's most wicked king. During his fifty-five-year reign, he brought the nation of Judah to its lowest point of depravity. He allowed—and participated in—setting up pagan altars and idols in the temple. Manasseh murdered prophets and innocent residents of Jerusalem (including his own children in a sacrificial fire to pagan gods), and he practiced sorcery and witchcraft. Perhaps this verse sums it up best:

> But Manasseh led the people of Judah and Jerusalem to do even more evil than the pagan nations whom the LORD had destroyed when the Israelites entered the land. (2 Chronicles 33:9)

The Lord captured Manasseh's attention, however, by allowing him to be captured by the Assyrians. That event humbled Manasseh, but his attempts at spiritual reform were too little too late, and they had no effect on reforming the immoral people of Judah. As you might expect, his son Amon followed the extended, degenerate example of his father instead of the short-lived repentant one. Speaking of short-lived, so was Amon, because he was assassinated by his own officials after ruling for only two years.

So this was the background of Zephaniah's prophecy. Blessings under the faithfulness of Hezekiah, but then the people went astray under Manasseh and Amon. But God was still willing to give Judah another chance. Judah was on a disaster course, heading straight for God's judgment—unless someone could change the direction of the nation. There wasn't much chance of that happening when Amon died and the throne was assumed by his eight-year-old son, Josiah.

But amazing things can happen when a leader seeks to follow God's direction.

The prepubescent King Josiah may have started his reign at a young age, but he quickly displayed more maturity than his father Amon:

- Josiah's coronation occurred in 638 B.C. when he was only eight years old.
- At the age of sixteen, he began to seek after God.
- When he was twenty, he began to purge the capital city of Jerusalem and the rest of Judah of its idols and pagan temples.
- While Assyria was preoccupied with fighting off the Babylonian invaders, Josiah expanded his influence to the north. The zealous young king swept through Palestine and demolished every altar to a foreign god he could find.
- In 620 B.C., at the age of twenty-six, Josiah began to repair the Temple in Jerusalem that had deteriorated from neglect and abuse during the reigns of Manasseh and Amon. A scroll was discovered in a dusty corner of the temple during the renovation. The priest, Hilkiah, determined that the scroll was a copy of the Law written by Moses (which had been lost in Jerusalem for decades). When the scroll was presented to Josiah, he began to read the Scriptures intently, and he insisted that they also be read to all of the people. This was the first time that Josiah learned of God's impending judgment:

When the king heard what was written in the Book of the Law, he tore his clothes in despair. Then he gave these orders to Hilkiah the priest . . . "Go to the Temple and speak to the LORD for me and for the people and for all Judah. Ask him about the words written in this scroll that has been found. The LORD's anger is burning against us because our ancestors have not obeyed the words in this scroll. We have not been doing what this scroll says we must do." (2 Kings 22:11–13)

- Josiah responded with even greater humility and reverence than before. The priestly ranks and temple services were soon back in order, and God told Josiah that God's hand of judgment would be withheld during Josiah's lifetime due to his humility before God.

• Josiah died at the age of thirty-eight after reigning as king for almost thirty-one years.

How is it that the boy-king, Josiah, would be so spiritually sensitive? Well, the prophet Zephaniah played a key role in all of that. Zephaniah's ministry took place during the reign of Josiah, and many scholars believe that Zephaniah had influence with the adolescent emperor. After all, as a coattail relative of royalty, Zephaniah probably enjoyed access to the palace. Zephaniah was a godly influence in the palace (maybe the only one in the early years of Josiah's reign), and the Lord used him to turn Josiah's heart toward God.

Now Hear This

Josiah's spiritual sensitivity, with his sense of repentance, was exactly the type of response that Zephaniah was after. Zephaniah had one message, and he never really digressed from it. He had a vision of world disaster, embracing both the outside world and the Jews. He identified the disaster as "the day of the Lord" and told the people to get ready for it. But as with the other prophets, his message of doom and gloom ended with the certainty of hope in God's redemption.

As one theologian has said, Zephaniah did not want to drive the people to despair, but he did want to drive them to God and to their duty. He didn't want to frighten them out of their wits, but he did want to frighten them out of their sins. He hammered them hard, but he wasn't interested in making them feel guilty; he simply wanted them to feel repentant. Like the guy in the rescue helicopter who shouted out a warning to you in our hypothetical illustration, Zephaniah shouted an urgent message to the people of Judah: "Disaster is heading your way unless you get serious about God." (This message also applies directly to us, but more about that later).

Perhaps more than any other of the Minor Prophets, Zephaniah declared that life without God is life without satisfaction. Even worse than that, life without God is life without a future. His brutal message was intended to convince the spiritually lethargic people of Judah that their God of holy hope was also a God of holy wrath. He wanted to impress upon them that their attitude, unless changed, would bring judgment upon them, with future hope for only a few of them who proved to be faithful in the end:

Their Attitude

Zephaniah preached that God is concerned about His people's rebellious attitude. He criticized the people of Judah because they did not obey God or those to whom God delegated His authority. He condemned them for their closed minds. They refused correction and rejected advice, and they exhibited a self-sufficient spirit. They felt no need to trust in the Lord, mistakenly believing that they could handle their own affairs. They continued to maintain a godly attitude on the outside—but as far as their hearts were concerned, they were disobedient. Although Josiah was sincere in his repentance and faithfulness, the great segment of the society was disinterested in God.

God's Judgment

Zephaniah predicted that God's judgment would be certain and that the punishment would be horrible. He said that God's awful wrath would obliterate everything in the land.

> "I will sweep away everything in all your land," says the LORD.
> "I will sweep away both people and animals alike. . . . I will reduce the wicked to heaps of rubble, along with the rest of humanity," says the LORD. (Zephaniah 1:2–3)

From the other prophets, the people knew that God would eventually bless them, but Zephaniah made it clear that there would be judgment first. He warned them that the great day of God's terrible judgment was approaching, and that it was coming very soon:

> That terrible day of the LORD is near. Swiftly it comes—a day when strong men will cry bitterly. It is a day when the LORD's anger will be poured out. It is a day of terrible distress and

anguish, a day of ruin and desolation, a day of darkness and
gloom, of clouds, blackness, trumpet calls, and battle cries.
(Zephaniah 1:14–16)

He was correct. The fearful wrath of God came on the nation relatively soon after he issued his warnings. By 605 B.C., only fifteen
years after Josiah began a revival with the discovery of the Temple
scroll, Judah was under the domination of Babylon. In that same
year, Jerusalem was invaded, and many of the city's young men were
enslaved and transported to the capital city of Babylonia. There was
a second invasion of Jerusalem in 597 B.C. when some ten thousand
Jews were deported. Finally, in 586 B.C., after a long siege by
Nebuchadnezzar, Jerusalem was finally destroyed.

The Future Hope

The book of Zephaniah is only three chapters long. That's a good
thing, because all of the disaster, doom, and despair of the first two
chapters can get really depressing. Fortunately, and almost surprisingly, the book ends on a high note in chapter 3. Zephaniah declares
that God's salvation and deliverance will be extended to those who
are faithful to Him:

> Sing, O daughter of Zion; shout aloud, O Israel! Be glad and
> rejoice with all your heart, O daughter of Jerusalem! For the
> LORD will remove his hand of judgment and will disperse the
> armies of your enemy. And the LORD himself, the King of
> Israel, will live among you! At last your troubles will be over,
> and you will fear disaster no more. (3:14–15)

Many Bible scholars believe Zephaniah is giving the reader a
glimpse into the millennial kingdom, when the Messiah will reign on
the earth in perfect peace and righteousness.

> For the LORD your God has arrived to live among you. He is
> a mighty savior. He will rejoice over you with great gladness.
> With his love, he will calm all your fears. He will exult over
> you by singing a happy song. (3:17)

They Just Didn't Care

Zephaniah's counsel and message penetrated the heart of Josiah, but it really didn't affect the people as a whole. Oh, sure, they responded to Josiah's spiritual reforms, but the change was purely superficial. There was no true sincerity in their actions. The people joined in the reforms initiated by Josiah simply because the king led them and not out of any real heart of repentance. (This was obvious when the people abandoned those spiritual reforms as soon as Josiah died.)

Zephaniah, speaking under the inspiration of the Holy Spirit, knew and understood that the outward appearance of reform was not produced by a true change of heart toward God. That is why the book of Zephaniah ignores the spiritual growth of Josiah and speaks of the people as being utterly corrupt. Zephaniah ignored the spiritual reforms that he knew to be insincere on the part of the people. Instead, He spoke only of the sin of the people and the swift judgment of God that was coming.

The people of Judah, and the residents of Jerusalem in particular, were supposed to be the magnets that drew the world to God; instead, they had lost all sense of spiritual commitment and had blended in with a pagan world. Zephaniah's sharpest criticism of them was directed at their spiritual indifference toward God:

> I will search with lanterns in Jerusalem's darkest corners to find
> and punish those who sit contented in their sins, indifferent to
> the LORD, thinking he will do nothing at all to them. (1:12)

The people of Judah assumed God's existence, but they had no conviction in their hearts that He really mattered. As far as they were concerned, He was either impotent or irrelevant. The NIV translation of Zephaniah 1:12 says that their thinking went something like this: "The LORD will do nothing, either good or bad."

They had become hardened and indifferent to God. The Jews at that time had such a low view of God that they believed He could not keep either His promises or His threats: He would do nothing, either good or bad. Their own spiritual complacency led them to think the Lord was complacent too.

Zephaniah knew that the people's spiritual indifference was the equivalent of practical atheism. Their errant lifestyle reflected a theology that believed:

- the Lord is there (in heaven) but not here (in daily life);
- the Lord is alive but not active;
- there is no reason to expect God's help or to fear His disapproval.

The people of Judah had no sorrow for their sins. They were prosperous, and they no longer cared about God. His demands for righteous living seemed irrelevant to the people, whose security and wealth made them complacent.

Spiritual Indifference Is Nothing to Wine About

Zephaniah knew that the nation's indifference toward God was the direct result of being spiritually stagnant. To make sure they understood the problem, he described their spiritual condition using a reference to the winemaking process. He reminded them that wine allowed to ferment for a long time forms a hard crust, and the liquid becomes syrupy, bitter, and unpalatable. Zephaniah used this analogy to describe the person who has lost all spiritual freshness and has instead stagnated in the monotony of comfort and luxury. Instead of removing the fermented and bitter spiritual pollution from their midst, the people of Judah wallowed in it. Their stagnant condition had curdled their concepts of God, their own souls, and eternity.

We Are Indifferent toward God (and That Ticks Him Off)

It is easy to be critical of the people of Judah for their feeble faith, but we might be guilty of the same sin. Think about it. Aren't we guilty, from time to time at least, of being indifferent toward God?

Like the people of Judah, we aren't atheists in our doctrine, but we come close to it in our daily lives. Practical atheism is not our professed creed, but it is the conviction of our hearts. We act as though the Lord is irrelevant. We proceed merrily along in our daily lives with no regard for Him. We have an intellectual knowledge that He exists somewhere "out there," but we sure don't act as if He is active (or relevant) to our lives "down here." We would never deny His existence, but we sure act as though He doesn't matter.

Are we being a bit too harsh on ourselves? We don't think so. It doesn't take a Zephaniah to see the signs of our indifference toward God. They are fairly obvious:

- If we really believed that God was powerful and relevant, wouldn't we be praying more?
- How come we are so tolerant of the immoral influence that exists in our society (that is projected into our living rooms from our television sets)?
- If we really believed that God responds to both righteousness and sin, wouldn't we be more serious about breaking our old sin habits?
- Wouldn't we be more grateful if we really believed that all of our provisions and resources were a gift from God (rather than what *we* earned through our own hard work)?
- Doesn't our lack of deep sorrow and repentance for our continual sin indicate indifference toward God?

Let's face it. Except for those periods of spiritual revival in our lives, we go through life with the calloused and complacent conviction that God is otiose. (We didn't know either. It means "idle, ineffective, useless, or superfluous." Accurate, don't you think?)

How So?

What is the reason for our spiritual indifference toward God? It may be a little different for each of us, but maybe our problem is the same as that of the people of Judah. Maybe it has to do with our material possessions. Nothing is more likely to lead people to be indifferent toward God than thinking they have no need of Him. As soon as we aren't worried about where our next meal is going to come from, we begin to get a false sense of independence. Relative comfort, combined with attitudes of self-sufficiency and indifference, lead us to mistakenly believe that God doesn't matter.

According to the Bible, wealth is not a vice any more than poverty is a virtue, but the Scripture asks three questions about wealth: How was it acquired? How is it being used? What is your attitude about your possessions?

That last question was the concern of Zephaniah. The people had so much laid up for themselves that they had been diverted from a sincere commitment to God. Don't let your prosperity, to whatever extent you have it, lead you to an attitude of prideful self-sufficiency.

Are You Ignoring the Warnings?

Is there a danger that you are spiritually indifferent? Has God brought a Zephaniah into your life? Is there a friend who is warning you about your spiritual complacency? Don't make the same mistake that the people of Judah did. Listen to what God is telling you:

> Fools think they need no advice, but the wise listen to others. (Proverbs 12:15)

> If you reject criticism, you only harm yourself; but if you listen to correction, you grow in understanding. (Proverbs 15:32)

Are you going to be like Judah and ignore Zephaniah's warnings?

> It proudly refuses to listen even to the voice of the LORD. No one can tell it anything; it refuses all correction. It does not trust in the LORD or draw near to its God. (3:2)

Or are you going to respond to them? If you are inclined to respond, then Zephaniah tells you how to do it. It is a simple two-step process.

STEP 1: Shut up and Listen!

Zephaniah believed that the severity of his message demanded that we come before the Lord in silent reverence and repentance:

> Stand in silence in the presence of the Sovereign LORD, for the awesome day of the LORD's judgment has come. (1:7)

Most of us could use a little sacred silence in our lives. Unfortunately, we don't do it very often, so it seems strange. We don't know what to be thinking while it is going on. If you are beginning to squirm uncomfortably after only a few milliseconds of silence in God's presence, you might find it helpful to focus your thoughts along these lines:

Adoration. You are in the presence of the Holy God of the universe.

> Be silent, and know that I am God. I will be honored by every nation. I will be honored throughout the world. (Psalm 46:10)

Contemplation. Give God a chance to reveal Himself in the wonder of the world around you.

> Stop and consider the wonderful miracles of God! (Job 37:14)

Expectation. Realize that God is ready, willing, and able to work in your life. What do you suppose He wants to do in your life?

> Be still in the presence of the LORD, and wait patiently for him to act. (Psalm 37:7)

Submission. Recognize that God's blessings will only be realized as you turn control of your life over to Him.

> Rescue me from my rebellion, for even fools mock me when I rebel. I am silent before you; I won't say a word. (Psalm 39:8–9)

Appreciation. Remember that God is all you have. Remember that God is all you need.

> I wait quietly before God, for my salvation comes from him. He alone is my rock and my salvation, my fortress where I will never be shaken. (Psalm 62:1–2)

STEP 2: Trust the Lord!

After you have given God the silent treatment, then it is time to get up and get moving—toward God. He should be the one in whom we place all of our trust and dependence. And if that is so, then we must lose our false pride and sense of self-sufficiency. We must approach God in humility:

> Those who are left will be the lowly and the humble, for it is they who trust in the name of the LORD. (Zephaniah 3:12)

Notice that Zephaniah didn't say that we have to clean up our acts before we go to God. It doesn't require a righteous résumé, just a repentant and submissive heart. Other religions say, "Become righteous, and then perhaps God will accept you." But the message of Zephaniah is that the only way to flee *from* sin is to flee *to* God. Absence of this earnest relationship invites condemnation, and this must now be put right with a spirit of humility and the intention of obedience.

Ask yourself these questions about your attitude toward God:

- Have I conquered my pride? Am I approaching God in humility or arrogance?
- Has there been a change in my inner life? Am I trying to obey His commandments?

> And how can we be sure that we belong to him? By obeying his commandments. (1 John 2:3)

Let us make every effort to bring God back into our lives. Otherwise, all we have is an empty religion in which God has no reality. Indifference makes a big difference.

CONSIDER HOW THINGS ARE GOING

Have you ever started a project with great enthusiasm, only to lose interest after a while? We all have. It's a characteristic of human nature to get all excited about something new, and it's just as natural to toss it aside or simply let it languish when something newer or more interesting comes along.

Sometimes dumping that old project is a good idea. For example, your goal to watch every Pauly Shore movie ever made seemed like a good idea at first, but after *Son-in-Law,* you gave up and moved on to something more worthwhile (which was just about anything else you could think of). That was a good idea.

On other occasions, giving up on your goal isn't so good, like the time you decided to dig your own backyard swimming pool by hand rather than pay "those ripoff artists with backhoes." After three weeks you gave up, and now your yard is an eyesore and a health hazard, and your neighbors aren't buying your explanation that a sinkhole mysteriously appeared in your yard last summer.

We have found through personal experience that it's always preferable to finish what we start. For one thing, our wives have an amazing ability to recite the abandoned projects that litter our lives. More important, goals that aren't completed can lead to discouragement, thereby hampering new and even more important things.

This is especially true when it comes to God's work. A lot of people think that all God cares about is that you start something spiritual— reading the Bible, attending church, witnessing to a neighbor, or teaching a Sunday school class—even if you never follow through.

Our intentions are what matter to God, and if for some reason our jobs or our families or some pressing matter takes our attentions away from Him and His work for a few months or years, that's OK. God understands. He doesn't expect us to give Him first place in every part of our lives, does He? As long as we have trusted Him for our eternal destiny, then the things we finish on earth aren't that important, as long as we do our best . . . right? Wrong.

Don't Even Start

Here's a little-known principle in Scripture: It's better not to start something of a spiritual nature in the first place than to start and not finish. Until we are ready to commit to finish the race, we shouldn't even run. Likewise, once we start running, we shouldn't stop until we cross the finish line.

Jesus told His disciples a story to illustrate this powerful principle:

> Don't begin until you count the cost. For who would begin construction of a building without first getting estimates and then checking to see if there is enough money to pay the bills? Otherwise, you might complete only the foundation before running out of funds. And then how everyone would laugh at you! They would say, "There's the person who started that building and ran out of money before it was finished!" (Luke 14:28–30)

What Was Jesus Thinking?

Jesus told this story as He walked through Jerusalem. He may have been thinking about the Temple, which had tremendous significance to Him. Jesus may have reflected on the glory of the first Temple, constructed by King Solomon nearly a thousand years earlier. More likely, given the nature of this story, He may have been thinking about the reconstruction project begun five hundred years earlier by the Jewish exiles, who had returned to Jerusalem after being held captive by the Babylonians for nearly seventy years.

Perhaps Jesus was thinking about the exiles' enthusiasm for rebuilding God's house under the supervision of Zerubbabel. They started the project with great fanfare but soon lost interest when other priorities got in the way. We don't know for sure if Jesus was reflecting on this particular piece of Jewish history, but we'd like to think that Jesus had it in mind when he said, "Count the cost."

The Prophet Haggai and the Temple of Gloom

The year was 520 B.C. The date: August 29. The place was Jerusalem. An unknown prophet by the name of Haggai began speaking to Zerubbabel, the governor of Judah, to Jeshua, the high priest, and through these two officials, to all the people. Here's what Haggai said:

> This is what the LORD Almighty says: The people are saying, "The time has not yet come to rebuild the LORD's house—the Temple." (1:2)

Unlike some of the other Minor Prophets, Haggai's message was very simple and straightforward. No one who heard it had to squint and ask, "Excuse me, would you please repeat that?" Governor Zerubbabel in particular knew exactly what the prophet was talking about.

You see, it had been only sixteen years since Zerubbabel had led fifty thousand Jewish exiles out of Babylon and back to Jerusalem. The Babylonians, led by King Nebuchadnezzar, had destroyed Jerusalem (including the Temple) and had captured the people of Judah in 586 B.C. But their conquest was short-lived. Just as the Lord had promised and the prophet Jeremiah had foretold, Babylon was conquered. The captivity of God's people was ended, and they were allowed to go home. Here's what God Himself said:

> "The truth is that you will be in Babylon for seventy years. But then I will come and do for you all the good things I have promised, and I will bring you home again. For I know the plans I have for you," says the LORD. "They are plans for good and not for disaster, to give you a future and a hope. In those days when you pray, I will listen. If you look for me in

earnest, you will find me when you seek me. I will be found by you," says the LORD. "I will end your captivity and restore your fortunes. I will gather you out of the nations where I sent you and bring you home again to your own land." (Jeremiah 29:10–14)

God accomplished this by raising up the kingdom of Persia to become the next great power, and He used King Cyrus, the Persian monarch. Cyrus issued a decree allowing the Jewish exiles to return to Jerusalem (Ezra 1:2–4). He even offered to finance the journey by returning the valuable items that King Nebuchadnezzar had taken from the Lord's Temple in Jerusalem and placed in the temple of his own gods (Ezra 1:7). Talk about poetic justice!

Everything Was Right Except . . .

Led by Zerubbabel and Jeshua, the exiles returned to Jerusalem and promptly began the work of rebuilding the Temple. This was their first priority. As John Montgomery Boice explained, these exiles and their leaders were the *right people* living in the *right place* wanting to do the *right thing* for the *right reasons*. The people gave God their all. They wanted to serve the God who had rescued them from captivity and restored their fortunes. They desired to put His work before their own interests.

The builders completed the foundation within two years of their arrival back in Jerusalem, prompting the people to sing praises to God:

> He is so good! His faithful love for Israel endures forever! (Ezra 3:11)

But then the work stopped. The people had intended to finish what they had started, but they encountered obstacles on two fronts:

The opposition planted seeds of doubt and discouragement. When the people of Israel returned to their own land, they found enemies who wanted their rebuilding project to fail, mainly because they wanted to keep Jerusalem from becoming strong once again. When these enemies couldn't disrupt the construction from within, they resorted to scare tactics and tried to discourage the builders.

We can expect opposition when we do God's work. "Yes, and everyone who wants to live a godly life in Christ Jesus will suffer persecution," wrote the apostle Paul (2 Timothy 3:12). <u>Discouragement and fear</u> are the biggest obstacles to finishing what we start for God, but they don't have to stop us. We can take comfort in the fact that this is nothing new, and that with God's help we can overcome and complete His will for us.

The government passed some new zoning laws. In 536 B.C., King Cyrus decreed that the Jewish exiles could return to their homeland. Then in 534 B.C. another Persian ruler, at the instigation of the enemies of Israel, passed a law that stopped construction on the Temple. Evidently Zerubbabel and the other leaders were not up on Persian law, or they would have known that a Persian decree could not be altered. Dr. Charles Feinberg wrote: "If faith had been present, the decree . . . would have been no deterrent in the work."[1] Instead the people were intimidated, and the work stopped. It wasn't until King Darius came to power that the phony decree was overturned and construction could begin once again. But by now it was 520 B.C. and the Temple had stood unfinished for fourteen years.

As God's people in our culture today, we need to respect the law and the government in power. But we also need to be aware when the opposition is encouraging lawmakers to enact bogus laws designed to limit our freedom to do God's work. We need skilled legislators, lawyers, and judges who will be advocates for fairness and equality under the law. There are many countries around the world where the rights of Christians to worship freely are severely restricted. We must never allow that to happen in our own land.

So here's the scene: It's been sixteen years since the rebuilding of God's Temple was started, fourteen since it stopped. No doubt the construction site has become an eyesore in the community and perhaps the object of ridicule. The good news is that the new king has given his consent for the rebuilding to continue, but there's some bad news as well, and it has nothing to do with the enemies of Israel or the government.

A Subtle Change

Over the last fourteen years something has happened, and God's not happy, but His reaction is very different from what we've seen before. He's not so much ticked off as greatly disappointed (sometimes that's worse). With the other Minor Prophets we've read how God approached His unrepentant people with warnings of what He would do if they didn't stop their evil ways. Here His approach is much more subtle, possibly because what has happened is very subtle. Remember, these were the *right people* living in the *right place* wanting to do the *right thing* for the *right reasons*. They weren't full of pride and they had not turned their backs on God. What they had done is to turn their attention to things other than God.

When the people began to rebuild the Temple, they put their hearts into the work and rejoiced as the foundation was laid. Then the opposition came, the project was shut down, and they put all of their energy toward other matters. As the years rolled by, they took on responsibilities, started families, built houses, and filled up their calendars—and they let the work of the Lord slide.

Notice in Haggai's book that the people didn't say they would never complete the Lord's house. The time just wasn't right (1:2). They weren't telling God, "No." They were simply saying, "God, we're too busy right now. Check back with us in a couple of years. We should be ready to resume Your work at that time."

Neglecting God's Work Doesn't Work

Can you believe the nerve of these people telling the one who rescued them from captivity, restored their fortunes, and returned them to their homeland that they were too busy to do His work? Yes you can, and so can we, because we have the same nerve.

God Is Ticked off When
We Neglect His Work

The people in Haggai's time thought they could divert their time and resources from God's work to their own affairs and get away with it, but they were wrong. It's no different for us.

Confessions of a Busy Christian

Remember when we were in college and single and we used to devote ourselves to the work of the church? Those Sunday night Bible studies were great. We used to bring our friends; some of them even got saved. Later we taught the second graders at church, and that was so much fun. Those kids sure have a heart for God. Then we started our careers, and we had to cut out some stuff. Hey, you've got to put your nose to the grindstone if you want to get ahead.

After we got married, we helped start a Bible study for young couples, but then the kids came along, and it was just so hard to get baby-sitters. Besides, we had to get involved in that soccer league, and isn't it a shame that they play those tournaments on Sundays? But that's the way it goes if you want to keep your kids happy.

We've had our ups and downs, but overall God has blessed us. We've been able to move into that new gated community, which is nice, but those mortgage payments are high. Now that the kids are in high school, we're both working, and that's tough. But what else can we do? We've got to pay the bills, and Jeff wants to go back east for school, and have you checked out the cost of college lately? Oh, and we just found out the Audi needs a new transmission.

Man, are we tired! It's like we're in one of those wheels in a rat's cage, spinning like crazy, using up all kinds of energy—getting nowhere. Someday we're going to slow down and get back to basics, to church, maybe take a short-term missions trip . . . someday.

Consider How Things Are Going

The approach Haggai used as he gave God's message to the leaders and the people of Israel was quite ingenious (what else would you expect when God is involved?). Rather than telling them what to expect in the future, Haggai asked them to do a self-assessment. "Consider how things are going for you!" he said emphatically. Variations of this phrase are used three times in this short book (1:5, 1:7, and 2:15). In effect he is saying, OK, you've done things your way for a few years now. You're living in luxury while the Lord's house lies in ruins (1:4). So how's it going? Well, let's make a list (1:6):

1. You've planted much but harvested little.
2. You have food to eat and wine to drink, but not enough to satisfy you.
3. You have clothing to wear, but it's not adequate for you.
4. You're making a decent wage, but inflation and expenses are eating you alive.

For all their effort to get ahead and build successful lives for themselves, the people had little to show for it. They worked hard but were never satisfied, echoing the words of mighty King Solomon:

> What do people get for all their hard work? Generations come and go, but nothing really changes. . . . Everything is so weary and tiresome! No matter how much we see, we are never satisfied. No matter how much we hear, we are not content. (Ecclesiastes 1:3–4, 8)

How Did This Happen?

You may be feeling like that right now. You're a good person. You aren't rebelling against God. You're just busy. Your excuse is that this condition is only temporary. You'll get to the things of God when you're not so busy and you don't have a corporate ladder to climb and a family to raise.

The problem is that, like the people of Israel, your priorities are inverted and you're not satisfied. Happiness comes and goes in your life, and joy is absent. There's an emptiness, and you don't know why.

How can this happen when your intentions are honorable? Plainly, God has allowed it to happen. He has allowed you to pursue your living because that's what you want, but because you have neglected His work, He has sent an emptiness that fills you like a disease.

> So he gave them what they asked for, but he sent a plague along with it. (Psalm 106:15)

> When God crosses our temporal affairs, and we meet with trouble and disappointment, we shall find the cause is, that the work we have to do for God and our own souls is left undone, and we seek our own things more than Christ.
>
> —Matthew Henry

How Do We Fix Things?

God is so good. He doesn't force us to do things His way. But when we don't, He does allow things to happen that will bring us to a point at which we have no choice but to consider how things are going. Then when we're ready to do things His way, He offers a solution. In Israel's case, it was very simple: Finish what you started:

> Now go up into the hills, bring down timber, and rebuild my house. Then I will take pleasure in it and be honored, says the LORD. (Haggai 1:8)

The same goes for us. Sometime in the past we started a relationship with God, and we eagerly did His work. We delighted in His Word, we eagerly worshiped Him with other believers, we talked to others about how much God meant to us, and we gave Him the first fruits of our labor. In short, we lived lives that were pleasing to God. But things have changed, and God is no longer pleased.

> But I have this complaint against you. You don't love me or each other as you did at first! Look how far you have fallen from your first love! Turn back to me again and work as you did at first. (Revelation 2:4–5)

That's where God wants us to start. He wants us to return to our first love, to turn back to Him so that He can restore to us again the joy of our salvation (Psalm 51:12).

God Responds When We Respond

Haggai is an encouraging book to read, and we think we know why. First, the people responded to God's message immediately. This isn't like some of the other Minor Prophet books, in which God's people continued to ignore Him. After considering their ways, Zerubbabel, Jeshua, and "the whole remnant of God's people obeyed the message from the LORD their God." And to show their intentions, "the people worshiped the LORD in earnest" (1:12).

True Worship

Don't confine your expression of worship to the time you stand up in church with your arms raised heavenward while the worship band plays the chorus to "Lord, I Lift Your Name on High" for the ninth time. Yes, worship involves singing praises, but it also involves active service to God, in which we give Him every part of our beings:

"I urge you therefore, brethren, by the mercies of God, to present your bodies a living and holy sacrifice, acceptable to God, which is your spiritual service of worship" (Romans 12:1 NASB).

This should encourage us to respond to God as well. Rather than thinking long and hard about doing the right thing, we can start right away. There's no interim period of evaluating our situation, wondering how extensively we should shift our priorities back to where God wants them. The whole issue isn't negotiable. We already know what the Lord requires of us (in case you've forgotten, go back and read Micah 6:8). All we have to do is respond.

The second bit of encouragement is that when we respond to God, He immediately responds to us. Haggai recorded that as soon as the people gave God their pledge of allegiance to God, He said, "I am with you!" (1:13). We get a picture of God letting out a big yell (like you do when your favorite football team scores the winning touchdown). God didn't look down on Zerubbabel like a vice principal who's just caught a punk without a hall pass. The text says, "So the LORD sparked the enthusiasm" of Zerubbabel and Jeshua to get back to work (1:14). God wasted no time in giving them the desire to finish the project.

But God wasn't finished. He had two more benefits for his people: God encouraged them when they got discouraged, and He promised to bless them. Both of these benefits apply to us as well when we devote ourselves to pleasing God by doing His will and His work.

God Will Be with Us

God understands when we get discouraged and feel defeated, which is going to happen when we devote ourselves to Him. What God offers is His encouragement and His presence. "Take courage and work, for I am with you, says the LORD Almighty" (Haggai 2:4). Matthew Henry wrote:

> Those who work for God have God with them; and if he be for us, who can be against us? This should stir us up to be diligent.

This is the promise God has given through the ages. When Moses was about to turn over the leadership of Israel to Joshua, the people were understandably nervous about their enemies. So Moses said, "Be strong and courageous! Do not be afraid of them! The LORD your God will go ahead of you. He will neither fail you nor forsake you" (Deuteronomy 31:6). When Joshua was in the heat of battle, he told the captains of his army: "Don't ever be afraid or discouraged. . . . Be strong and courageous, for the LORD is going to do this to all of your enemies" (Joshua 10:25).

When David was about to turn over the reins of the kingdom to his son Solomon, he said: "Be strong and courageous, and do the work. Don't be afraid or discouraged by the size of the task, for the LORD God, my God, is with you. He will not fail you or forsake you" (1 Chronicles 28:20). And when Paul gave advice on how to fight against the evil rulers and authorities of the unseen world, he wrote: "Be strong with the Lord's mighty power" (Ephesians 6:10).

We can take courage because God is with us. "My Spirit remains among you," He promised the people of Israel (Haggai 2:5), and the same goes for us. We have God's power because we have God's presence, and when we have His presence, we have His help, protection, and blessing. There's nothing more powerful than this:

> If God is for us, who can ever be against us? (Romans 8:31)

God Will Bless Us

The second benefit of devoting ourselves to pleasing God by doing His will and doing His work follows the first: When God is with us, He automatically blesses us. Dr. Charles Feinberg wrote:

> Blessed is the lot of that people that yields to the leading of the Lord to do his work in his appointed time. Blessing must follow.[2]

Don't expect some kind of material blessing just because you decide to devote yourself to God. God has a much bigger blessing in mind for you. Think about what you get when you put your own work first: trouble, frustration, and disappointment. Now think about what you get when you put God's work first: peace, joy, and purpose. That's the blessing of God, and there's no amount of money in the world that can buy it. Oh, the material blessings will come, but only when we trust the Lord for His provision.

This is where true faith comes in. Are we willing to back off from our busy schedules and the relentless pursuit of success in order to put God and His work first? We're not talking about quitting your job, selling the house, and moving to Outer Mongolia. Your career is not His primary concern—He wants your heart.

The urge to look out for yourself and your family will still be there, even after you decide to follow Christ fully, so you have to remind yourself of what it was like when you did it your way. Remember back to the trouble, frustration, and disappointment. Recall how unfulfilling it all was. Then realize that God wants you to draw a line in the sand. He wants you to change the way you live and put Him first.

God made a specific promise on a specific day to the people of Israel, and it required faith for them to accept it:

> On this eighteenth day of December—the day when the foundation of the LORD's Temple was laid—carefully consider this: I am giving you a promise now while the seed is still in the barn, before you have harvested your grain and before the grapevine, the fig tree, the pomegranate, and the olive tree

have produced their crops. From this day onward I will bless you. (Haggai 2:18–19)

How about you? Are you willing to put God first before you get that raise, before the stock market goes back up, before you've paid for the kids' college educations? Are you willing to put God to the test and change your priorities now, before your ship comes in?

> He is no fool who gives what he cannot keep to gain what he cannot lose.
>
> —Jim Elliot

Change Your Priorities Now

Jesus addressed the issue of priorities when He was on a mountain teaching His disciples. In Matthew 6, Jesus talked about money, faith, and priorities. Here are some excerpts:

> No one can serve two masters. For you will hate one and love the other, or be devoted to one and despise the other. You cannot serve both God and money. (v. 24)

> So don't worry about having enough food or drink or clothing. Why be like the pagans who are so deeply concerned about these things? Your heavenly Father already knows all your needs, and he will give you all you need from day to day if you live for him and make the Kingdom of God your primary concern. (v. 31–33)

Kingdom Living Now

As this chapter comes to a close, we want to focus on Jesus' advice to "make the Kingdom of God your primary concern." In this little piece of advice, Jesus summarized what it takes to put the will and work of God first in your life: We need to rearrange our priorities so God is on top. It's not enough to acknowledge God as our Lord and Savior. We need to change our calendars. We need to refocus our efforts so that the work of God supersedes our work, trusting God to give us all we need when we need it.

Jesus also encouraged his disciples to invest in the work of the Lord, because "the purses of heaven have no holes in them" (Luke 12:33). What a contrast from the pockets of earth that are full of holes (Haggai 1:6). "Wherever your treasure is, there your heart and thoughts will also be," Jesus said (Luke 12:34). If we want to set our hearts on things above, we need to rearrange our priorities.

Kingdom Living Then

There's another aspect to kingdom living, and that's recognizing the future kingdom of God. As the people of Israel got back to the business of rebuilding the Temple of God, they became discouraged because their little construction project paled in comparison to the way the Temple was before. God recognized this, and He told them to have courage and keep going, because someday there would be a temple filled with God's glory that would be greater than any temples of the past. This must have filled the people of God with hope.

We can find hope in this as well. Someday all that we have done on earth will be gone, except for the things we did for God. As the old saying goes: "Only one life, 't'will soon be passed; only what's done for Christ will last."

All of the present kingdoms will someday pass away, but the kingdom of God will reign forever. Someday all of the temples made by human hands will be gone, but the Lord will be in His holy Temple, and we will worship Him forever.

> Since we are receiving a Kingdom that cannot be destroyed, let us be thankful and please God by worshiping him with holy fear and awe. (Hebrews 12:28)

PHONY BALONEY

As you can imagine, writing a book about the messages of the Minor Prophets is an overwhelming task. After all, it requires knowledge of ancient Hebrew to be able to translate the texts of the Minor Prophets from their original language into English. We don't have that knowledge, of course, but we read the books and commentaries written by scholars who know all about ancient Hebrew. (We had a tough enough time trying to understand what they had written in English.)

We have come to learn that Bible translation is both an art and a science. It involves history, archeology, and linguistics. From an ancient document, the translators ascertain the exact wording of what was written, but then they need to understand the cultural setting and historical references in which it was written to determine the exact meaning. Then those concepts are put into our contemporary English language so that the translation is accurately conveyed to us. And the nuances of our language keep changing, so they have to be fluent in both the ancient languages and the modern ones.

Sometimes Bible translators get stuck with an ancient word that doesn't really have a contemporary equivalent. Other times they get lucky because the ancient word has a meaning that is well-known in our culture, with lots of synonyms to choose from. In this chapter, we will be dealing with one of those words that is well-known throughout all time and by all peoples regardless of their cultures: *hypocrisy*.

You can guess what comes next:

GOD IS TICKED OFF BY OUR HYPOCRISY

The Bible talks a lot about the sin of hypocrisy. Because hypocrisy is a worldwide sin, known in every society, this is not a difficult concept for Bible scholars to translate into English or any other language. For example, there is a remote Indian tribe in Latin America that uses several different phrases to describe a person who is a hypocrite. In their dialect, such a person is referred to as having two faces or two hearts, being two-headed, or having a straight mouth but a crooked heart.

We know you can relate to these characterizations of hypocrisy because that is how the term is used in our culture as well. There is a bifurcated aspect to the personal nature of every hypocrite. They say one thing, but they do another. Or their outward actions are contrary to their inward beliefs. You can't trust them because what you see is *not* what you get with them.

Have you ever noticed that the term *hypocrisy* is usually raised in the context of religion or a person's spiritual beliefs? The term accurately applies in many situations, but we only use it when the phoniness relates to faith or religious conviction. We have "a hypocrite" for religion, and use other terms for everything else. For example:

- If a business executive breaks a promise, he or she is described as being "ruthless."
- If a person claims to be your friend and then spreads gossip about you, that person is "disloyal."
- A politician who is elected as a Democrat but then continually votes with the Republicans is labeled a "traitor."
- If your child acts like an angel while you are watching but immediately disobeys when you leave the room, the child is a "manipulator."

But put the same type of duplicitous behavior in the context of religion, and you've got a hypocrite. In fact, one of the principal definitions of hypocrisy is couched in church terminology: You are a hypocrite if you don't practice what you preach. Preaching isn't done by corporate executives or friends or politicians or kids. Preaching falls exclusively within the purview of religious people. Apparently, so does hypocrisy.

We don't blame society for tweaking the definition of hypocrisy a bit so that it gets used primarily in the context of religion. After all, some of the greatest examples of the term have been televangelists and high-profile ministers who chastised and condemned the nation for its immoral behavior. These sanctimonious charlatans were later exposed for their own sins (which usually involved exposure of a different type). It's one thing to be a fraud—we all are to one extent or another—but it is worse if you are ensnared by sin while you seek fame (and billions of bucks from tax-deductible contributions) on the premise that you have achieved a moral superiority that others lack.

But Christian hypocrites aren't only found behind the pulpit or in front of the television camera. The pews are full of them. And for most of us, that is where we gain personal, firsthand knowledge of the offense of hypocrisy. You hear those self-righteous pew sitters rattle on every Sunday about their holy lives, but you know that they spend Monday through Saturday being petty and dishonest. If you are like us (and we hope you aren't), it is all you can do to contain yourself and refrain from stuffing their Bibles down their throats.

Isn't it ironic that the religious hypocrite is pretending to be something that he or she is not, while everyone knows that this is just a spiritual act put on for their benefit? All of that pretending doesn't fool anyone. We heard the story of a hypocritical woman who thought she had the people of her church fooled. At every opportunity for her to pray aloud, she proclaimed the depth of her faith with majestic phrases, speaking with vocabulary that was a mix of the King James Bible and Shakespeare. During one of her prayers, she raised her voice and implored: "Heavenly Father, because I desire that you continueth your sanctifying work within me, I ask that you filleth me with your Holy Spirit." One church member could stand the hypocrisy no longer and interjected, "Oh, Lord, don't do it! She leaks!"

If you are irritated by spiritual hypocrisy, try to imagine how much God dislikes it. After all, He is the one that hypocrites pretend to love. But their hypocrisy means that they are more concerned about their own image than the God they are supposedly in love with. The Bible makes it very clear that God sees right through our hypocrisy, and that He doesn't care for it at all.

- King David warned that hypocrites should be avoided because they are a bad influence (Psalm 26:4).
- The prophet Isaiah says that God considers the worship of a hypocrite to be worthless (Isaiah 29:13).
- Jesus publicly rebuked the religious leaders and Pharisees for their spiritual hypocrisy (Matthew 23:27–28).
- The apostle Paul referred to hypocrites as being despicable and disobedient (Titus 1:16).
- And Peter, who had a few hypocritical tendencies of his own from time to time, knew from personal experience that it should be avoided at all costs (1 Peter 2:1).

These passages are enlightening, but they don't tell us all we need to know. You see, God just doesn't consider spiritual hypocrisy to be an unfortunate character deficiency. He hates it. As you will soon see from the message of Zechariah, spiritual hypocrisy ticks God off.

Construction Cheerleader with a Vision

If you read chapter 10 about Haggai, then you already know the historical context of Zechariah. And you should have no problem remembering what you read, because it was only four pages ago, and we are sure that you have been so spellbound that you haven't put this book down since you first encountered Hosea and Gomer in chapter 1. But on the off chance that some disaster demanded your attention immediately after reading chapter 10—like a ruptured appendix or a surprise visit from your in-laws—allow us to refresh your memory.

In 586 B.C., the armies of Babylon invaded Jerusalem and destroyed the Temple. This was the final decimation of the southern kingdom of Judah, and thousands of Jews were taken captive and shipped off to live in Babylon. Only the weak and the impoverished were left behind, the vestiges of a once-great nation gone.

Under the rule of King Cyrus, Persia overthrew the Babylonian Empire in 539 B.C. With a little help from God's Spirit, Cyrus encouraged the Jews who were living in Babylon to return to Jerusalem and rebuild their city (and God's temple). About fifty thousand exiles headed back to Jerusalem in 538 B.C.

As with most building projects, there was a lot of excitement at first. As the city of Jerusalem was repopulated, work began on the Temple. Within two years, the foundation had been laid, and an altar had been built for offering sacrifices to God. However, due to external opposition and internal depression, the people's enthusiasm waned and the work came to a halt. In fact, enthusiasm for the task completely evaporated because no progress was made for more than a decade. It seems that the people were more concerned with their own homes than with the house of the Lord.

Then Haggai spoke up in 520 B.C. He must have been a great motivational speaker (which often happens as a direct result of speaking the words of God) because the people immediately returned to the task of rebuilding the Temple.

There! Now it all came back to you.

Zechariah was born in Babylon. As a kid, he was one of the fifty thousand refuges who returned to Jerusalem in 538 B.C. He began his career as a prophet in the fall of 520 B.C. A mere two months after Haggai assumed the role of construction cheerleader, Zechariah picked up a pair of pompoms and joined the pep squad.

Zechariah was much younger than Haggai, so Zechariah had the stamina to be much more long-winded and verbose with his cheering. Haggai kept his cheering short, crisp, and to the point: "Build the Temple!" Zechariah also shouted encouragement to rebuild the Temple, but he went on to explain that it was an important step in God's plan for the glorious future that awaits God's people when the Messiah will reign on Earth.

It is difficult to work messianic prophesies into construction cheers, but that is exactly what Zechariah did. Except for Isaiah, Zechariah has more references about the coming Messiah than any other prophet (Major or Minor). The last half of the book is focused exclusively on the Messiah's future role of breaking the barriers between Jews and Gentiles and making God's salvation available to the human race. Zechariah had two "oracles" that were probably recorded later in his life. The first oracle describes aspects of what will happen when the Messiah comes to earth the first time (when He would be rejected by Israel); the second oracle describes the

Second Coming of the Messiah, when He will establish His kingdom on Earth.

As twenty-first-century Christians, we have the advantages of time and history that weren't available to Zechariah or the people who heard him prophesy. We know that Jesus Christ was the Messiah, and that His first coming resulted in His crucifixion and resurrection. We don't have to stretch the predictions of the prophets to match Jesus with the identity of the Messiah. Jesus, and only Jesus, has fulfilled the hundreds of predictions that were made about His identity as the Messiah. If our faith ever waivers, all we need to do is to remind ourselves that guys like Zechariah predicted details about the Messiah more than five hundred years before Christ was born. These details included predictions that during His first coming He would make a victorious entry through the gates of Jerusalem—not riding on a charging white horse as was the tradition, but on a donkey's colt. We know this event as Palm Sunday, but Zechariah only knew it as his vision of the future when he said:

> Rejoice greatly, O people of Zion! Shout in triumph, O people of Jerusalem! Look, your king is coming to you. He is righteous and victorious, yet he is humble, riding on a donkey— even a donkey's colt. (Zechariah 9:9)

Because Jesus fulfilled all of the prophecies about the Messiah's First Coming, we can take great assurance that He will fulfill all of the prophecies about the Messiah's Second Coming.

> And the LORD will be king over all the earth. On that day there will be one LORD—his name alone will be worshiped. (Zechariah 14:9)

A Brutal Answer to a Seemingly Innocent Question

Sandwiched between eight visions about Israel's secure future in the Lord (chapters 1–6) and prophecies about the First and Second

Comings of the Messiah (chapters 9–14), Zechariah gives a word from God that hit the people like a sucker-punch. They never saw it coming. They thought they were going to get a few answers about ritual protocol, but Zechariah hit them with God's righteous indignation.

The Jews continued to return to their homeland from Babylon over the years since the first resettlement trek of 538 B.C., but all of them didn't go for life in the big city. Instead of choosing Jerusalem, many of them picked the more rural settings of the outlying region. Bethel was one of those villages located about twelve miles north of Jerusalem. At a time when the Temple was about halfway completed, a small delegation of leaders from Bethel went to Jerusalem to ask Zechariah a technical question about one of the fasting rituals.

A Fast Course on Fasting

God had given Moses instructions about instituting certain annual commemorative events and celebrations. In addition, over the centuries, the Jews had added a few of their own. And during the Babylonian exile, the people imposed and practiced a few fasting days to memorialize past events of hardship and suffering (all connected with punishment for their sins):

- They fasted during the fourth month to remember the conquest of Jerusalem by Nebuchadnezzar.
- There was a fast on the seventh day of the fifth month to remember the destruction of the temple when Nebuchadnezzar burned it to the ground on that day in 586 B.C.
- They fasted for a day in the seventh month to commemorate the murder of Gedaliah, a Judean governor.
- There was a fast in the tenth month to observe the initial attack and first siege of Jerusalem by Nebuchadnezzar.

With the Temple being rebuilt, and since construction was about 50 percent completed, it seemed innocent enough to ask whether the people should still fast for a day in the fifth month to mourn the destruction of the Temple approximately seventy years before. After all, the people from the village of Bethel were somewhat removed from the religious hierarchy in Jerusalem, but they could probably see the Temple reconstruction from a distance. How would they know the rules unless they asked?

> The people of Bethel had sent Sharezer and Regemmelech, along with their men, to seek the LORD's favor. They were to ask this question of the prophets and of the priests at the Temple of the LORD Almighty: "Should we continue to mourn and fast each summer on the anniversary of the Temple's destruction, as we have done for so many years?" (Zechariah 7:2–3)

That's an honest question, isn't it? But before we get to Zechariah's response, let's consider a few things:

First, some Bible scholars explain that the phrase "seek the Lord's favor" means that they were expecting a response that would let them off the hook from continuing this fast in the future. That makes their bland question seem a bit more like: "We don't have to keep doing this fast thing, do we?"

And second, the delegation only had a vague recollection of the period during which they had observed this fast. They said that they had been doing it "for so many years." Some scholars read into this phrase the fact that the delegation didn't really remember, or even know, the date of the Temple's destruction. The event had lost its significance and they had grown weary of the required ritual.

Spiritual Hypocrisy Exposed

Zechariah didn't hold back in responding to the question posed to him by the Bethel delegation. But his initial response wasn't a direct answer to their question. Instead, he accused them of spiritual superficiality and hypocrisy. And because these words were so harsh, Zechariah made sure that everyone knew that he wasn't giving a personal opinion but was speaking the words of the Lord:

> The LORD Almighty sent me this message: "Say to all your people and your priests, 'During those seventy years of exile, when you fasted and mourned in the summer and at the

festival in early autumn, was it really for me that you were fasting? And even now in your holy festivals, you don't think about me but only of pleasing yourselves. (Zechariah 7:4–6)

This was a double-barreled blast at their hypocrisy. God wasn't at the center of their celebrations. Their religious rituals were a sham. They cared only about appearing to be devoted to God, but there was no genuine interest in God at all. The rituals were performed without even thinking about Him. Instead, they thought only about how they looked to others, and how good they felt about themselves for being so "holy." God was irrelevant.

Zechariah smacked them with the reality that their lives lacked genuine spirituality, and reminded them of the kind of conduct that pleases God:

> Then this message come to Zechariah from the LORD: "This is what the LORD Almighty says: Judge fairly and honestly, and show mercy and kindness to one another." (7:8–9)

God is ticked off when we pretend that we love Him but don't know what is important to Him. That was the failing of the Israelites throughout much of their history. They played a good religious game, but they were totally out of it as far as God was concerned. Their religious hypocrisy caused them to focus so much on themselves that they became immune to God's conviction through the message of the prophets. Zechariah didn't want his people to suffer from the same fate:

> Your ancestors would not listen to this message. They turned stubbornly away and put their fingers in their ears to keep from hearing. They made their hearts as hard as stone, so they could not hear the law or the messages that the LORD Almighty had sent them by his Spirit through the earlier prophets. That is why the LORD Almighty was so angry with them. (7:11–12)

Zechariah's message to the people was clear: Fasts or no fasts, it doesn't really matter. Formality is meaningless if there is no reality behind it. And insincerity and hypocrisy make God angry, so you'd better make every effort to live your life with genuine righteousness.

Because the people had been duplicitous, deceitful, and dishonest for so long, Zechariah reminded them what their conduct should look like:

> But this is what you must do: Tell the truth to each other. Render verdicts in your courts that are just and that lead to peace. Do not make evil plots to harm each other. And stop this habit of swearing to things that are false. I hate all these things, says the LORD. (8:16–17)

Just in case you are wondering, Zechariah finally got around to answering their question directly. He said that those mournful fasts should be turned into times of joy and celebration. But the real cause for celebration—and what would bring them genuine peace—would be sincere worship and love of God:

> Here is another message that came to me from the LORD Almighty. "This is what the LORD Almighty says: The traditional fasts and times of mourning you have kept in early summer, midsummer, autumn, and winter are now ended. They will become festivals of joy and celebration for the people of Judah. So love truth and peace. (8:18–19)

Denying Our Spiritual Hypocrisy

Zechariah's message to the people of Bethel was intended to be a criticism and a wake-up call to all of the Jews. Similarly, Zechariah's message is intended for us as well. We need to examine the sincerity of our own spiritual conditions. And the mistakes of ancient Israel should be a lesson and a warning for us today:

> All these events happened to them as examples for us. They were written down to warn us, who live at the time when this age is drawing to a close. If you think you are standing

strong, be careful, for you, too, may fall into the same sin.
(1 Corinthians 10:11–12)

God doesn't change. The attitudes that He required of the people twenty-five hundred years ago, He requires of us now. He loves the same things. He hates the same things. And what He hated then and now is spiritual hypocrisy.

We know God hates insincerity, dishonesty, and deceit in our lives. That is exactly what we are guilty of when we pretend to be spiritual but we are not. If we are putting on a show of Christian commitment but lack a heart that longs for God, then those "good deeds" are meaningless. If fact, they offend God because they are performed out of our own pride (to make ourselves feel good or to impress others) instead of being done as an act of worship. At best, such conduct reveals a lack of true love for God; at worst, it reflects contempt for Him.

As contemporary Christians, we don't have all of the rituals and traditions that caused the Jews to be legalistic, trapped in spiritual hypocrisy. Or do we? The people in your church and in your circle of Christian friends have certain expectations of what a "good Christian" does (and doesn't do), don't they? Many Christians feel some pressure to live up to expectations in the areas of:

- church attendance
- reading the Bible on a daily basis
- spending time with God in prayer each day
- giving 10 percent of your paycheck to the Lord's work
  (although you may have the personal freedom to decide
  whether the 10 percent comes off the gross or net pay)

All these activities are commended in Scripture because all of them are beneficial to our spiritual growth. But if we are honest with ourselves, we must admit that much of the time we do them (or pretend that we do them) for the sake of appearance rather than out of a genuine love for the Lord.

Let's use the warning issued by Zechariah as an opportunity to examine ourselves for the symptoms of spiritual hypocrisy.

Hypocrites are more concerned about the traditions of humans than about the truths of God. We have many sacred traditions in our faith, but they shouldn't be what motivate us. Traditions done merely as a ritual can mask a heart that is cold toward God. That is the criticism that Jesus dumped on the Pharisees:

> You like to look good in public, but God knows your evil hearts. What this world honors is an abomination in the sight of God. (Luke 16:15)

Usually, we are more concerned about our performance than God's principles. But we've got it backward. We should care more about God's truth and less about our behavior. When we make God's truth our primary focus and constant motivation, then our perform-ance will be properly aligned with those divine principles.

Hypocrites are more worried about their outward appearance than their inward condition. Jesus gave His disciples a classic illustration of spiritual hypocrisy:

> Two men went to the Temple to pray. One was a Pharisee, and the other was a dishonest tax collector. The proud Pharisee stood by himself and prayed this prayer: "I thank you, God, that I am not a sinner like everyone else, especially like that tax collector over there! For I never cheat, I don't sin, I don't commit adultery, I fast twice a week, and I give you a tenth of my income."
>
> But the tax collector stood at a distance and dared not even lift his eyes to heaven as he prayed. Instead, he beat his chest in sorrow, saying, "O God, be merciful to me, for I am a sinner." I tell you, this sinner, not the Pharisee, returned home justified before God. (Luke 18:10–14)

The Pharisee in this story was doing good things, but he was doing them for the sake of recognition of the people around him. He knew that they couldn't see into his heart; they could only evaluate him based on the things that they saw him do. But God uses a dif-ferent standard of analysis:

The LORD doesn't make decisions the way you do! People judge by outward appearance, but the LORD looks at a person's thoughts and intentions. (1 Samuel 16:7)

God knows the condition of our hearts. If we are serious about our commitment to Him, we'd better stop worrying about our reputations and start getting serious about what is going on inside our hearts.

I know all the things you do, and that you have a reputation for being alive—but you are dead. Now wake up! Strengthen what little remains, for even what is left is at the point of death. Your deeds are far from right in the sight of God. (Revelation 3:1–2)

Hypocrites are intent about the insignificant things but ignore the indispensable ones. Sometimes we make a big deal about things that aren't really important to God. We might be worried about whether we should pray over the meal in a restaurant while God is more concerned about our lack of love for our neighbors.

When King Saul bragged about pleasing the Lord by making sacrifices, the prophet Samuel confronted Saul's hypocrisy:

What is more pleasing to the LORD: your burnt offerings and sacrifices or your obedience to his voice? Obedience is far better than sacrifice. Listening to him is much better than offering the fat of rams. Rebellion is as bad as the sin of witchcraft, and stubbornness is as bad as worshiping idols. (1 Samuel 15:22–23)

Hypocrites are more interested in rules than in repentance. If you like to-do lists, then you probably like religious rituals. You can put them on a list and check them off when you are done with them. But the keeping of rules and rituals are no substitute for genuine godliness.

Our lives before God should reflect genuine repentance and humility. This won't happen if we take selfish pride in accomplishing everything on our Christian to-do lists. Having our devotions, placing a check in the offering basket, and teaching the Sunday-school class are meaningless if we have an arrogant attitude. An attitude of submission should always precede acts of service.

> So humble yourselves before God. Resist the Devil, and he will flee from you. Draw close to God, and God will draw close to you. Wash your hands, you sinners; purify your hearts, you hypocrites. Let there be tears for the wrong things you have done. Let there be sorrow and deep grief. Let there be sadness instead of laughter, and gloom instead of joy. When you bow down before the LORD and admit your dependence on him, he will lift you up and give you honor. (James 4:7–10)

Hypocrites do the right things for the wrong reasons. Just because you are doing something good doesn't mean that what you are doing is acceptable in God's eyes. God doesn't consider your conduct to be at all worthy if your attitude is all wrong. Regardless of how "religious" they may seem to others, your actions aren't right before God if your attitude isn't righteous.

> Dear brothers and sisters, the longing of my heart and my prayer to God is that the Jewish people might be saved. I know what enthusiasm they have for God, but it is misdirected zeal. For they don't understand God's way of making people right with himself. Instead, they are clinging to their own way of getting right with God by trying to keep the law. They won't go along with God's way. For Christ has accomplished the whole purpose of the law. All who believe in him are made right with God. (Romans 10:1–4)

Zechariah had a two-pronged message that has remained relevant through the centuries: 1) God is ticked off by spiritual hypocrisy, and 2) if we say we love God, we'd better mean it. While the world may judge our spirituality by our actions, God know our attitudes as well.

WHAT GOD WANTS TO DO

Until recently we didn't think it was all that important to have a thorough knowledge of history. Like most people, we treated history like algebra: You need to take it in school, but there's not much practical use for it. As long as you know a few basics and memorize some key dates (1492, 1812, 1944, etc.), you can get by just fine.

Then we began to research and write this book on the Minor Prophets, and we realized that our casual treatment of past events and people was a big mistake. History may seem like a dry and dusty subject to most of us, but it doesn't have to be; not when we understand that God is a God of history. Even though God is not bound by time, He created time when He created the universe, and when He created time, He created history. So in effect, to ignore history is to ignore what God has done, and none of us wants to do that.

When you realize that God is a God of history, all kinds of new ideas come to you; for example, the idea that history is under God's control. Though it may not always seem like it, history is following God's divine plan and timetable. Just because the world is not the way God intended it, don't think for a minute that He has lost control. History is headed to a divine conclusion, and we are part of it.

You find this stuff out when you read the Bible as a history book, which it is. You could say it's God's story ("his story"—get it?) of what He has done and continues to do to establish a personal relationship with mankind. This became especially clear when we tackled Malachi, the last Minor Prophet and the last book in the Old Testament. More than any other book in the Bible, Malachi is sandwiched between past and future events; between what God has already done and what He is going to do. The lessons we can learn from this book are significant, because they center on God's faithfulness in the past and our hope for the future.

History Lessons

Of course, Malachi is first and foremost a story of God dealing with His people, the Jews, but it goes beyond that. There are applications for us today, and they are just as fresh and relevant as they were when Malachi wrote his book in 430 B.C.

In order to get a context for Malachi's book, we need to get a perspective on the history of the times (somehow you knew this was coming). Now, don't skip this part, because it will help you understand Malachi's message. Besides, this will serve as a review of some of the stuff we've talked about in previous chapters. Here are a few key dates and events (don't worry, there won't be a test later):

597 B.C. Babylon came to power with King Nebuchadnezzar at the helm. This is also the year the Babylonians captured Jerusalem.

586 B.C. Nebuchadnezzar destroyed Jerusalem and carried off the Jews into exile.

538 B.C. Persia, under the rule of King Cyrus, conquered Babylon.

536 B.C. Cyrus allowed fifty thousand exiles to return to their homeland under the leadership of Zerubbabel, the governor of Judah. The exiles began rebuilding the Temple, but stopped after two years.

520 B.C. After sixteen years building up their own houses at the expense of God's house, Zerubbabel and the people listened to the prophets Haggai and Zechariah and resumed work on the Temple.

516 B.C. The building was completed at the time of Passover, and the priestly ministry was reestablished.

458 B.C. A second migration of exiles from Babylon returned to Jerusalem under the leadership of Ezra the scribe.

446 B.C. Nehemiah, the Jewish cupbearer of the Persian king, heard a report about the conditions in Palestine and

Jerusalem. The wall of Jerusalem had been broken down and the gates had been burned. Nehemiah took up the challenge of traveling to Jerusalem to repair the damage. In less than two months he gets the job done.

430 B.C. Malachi becomes a prophet and gives the last message the people will hear from God for more than four hundred years.

Did You Know?

The Greek historian Herodotus wrote the world's first comprehensive book of history (called *History*, oddly enough) in 430 B.C., at the exact same time Malachi was writing his book.

From the perspective of history, we can see how utterly faithful God was in protecting, preserving, and providing for His people. The children of Israel could see this too, but for some reason they didn't trust God. And since they didn't trust God, they weren't obeying God. Nehemiah instituted some effective reforms among the people, but they didn't last. By the time Malachi came on the scene, the people had sunk into serious moral and spiritual decline. They were willing to accept God's provision but unwilling to follow His will.

What Ticks God Off

Why did the children of Israel fail to trust God for the future in light of His faithfulness in the past? Was it because they were tired of waiting for the promised Messiah? Were they concerned that God was not going to punish their enemies? Did they think God had abandoned them? Had they begun to question God's love for them?

If you think the Israelites were thickheaded, you're right. But don't get smug about it. Aren't we the same way? Don't we sometimes wonder if Jesus is really going to come back to earth? Aren't we frustrated that godless people and nations are getting away with murder?

If we are completely honest, don't we sometimes question God's love for us, especially when things aren't going so well?

The problem is that we shift the focus away from God and direct it to ourselves. It's all about us, isn't it? No matter how much God has done for us in the past, we want to know what He's going to do next. And meanwhile, we fail to follow what God wants us to do right now. As Matthew Henry wrote, "We all are prone to undervalue the mercies of God, and to excuse our own offences."[1]

That combination of underestimating God and overestimating ourselves leads to something that ticks God off:

GOD IS TICKED OFF BY OUR APATHY

Whatever the reasons for Israel's shortsighted behavior, they had become apathetic in their relationship with God. Even worse, they had become arrogant about their own self-reliance and skeptical about God's faithfulness. They even had the nerve to question God when He sent Malachi to get them back on track. So God let them have it. He told them exactly why He was ticked off and, like the merciful and loving God He is, He told them exactly what to do about it.

As you read Malachi's message, you can see that God's people were blowing it in three different areas. Evidently we haven't learned from history, because we continue to tick God off in these same areas today.

How We Treat God

Malachi's message starts off in a much different tone than the other Minor Prophets. In every other book, God wasted no time in expressing His anger. Here's a sampling:

> Get up and go to the great city of Nineveh! Announce my judgment against it because I have seen how wicked its people are. (Jonah 1:2)

> The LORD is a jealous God, filled with vengeance and wrath. (Nahum 1:2)

I will sweep away everything in all your land. (Zephaniah 1:2)

I, the LORD, was very angry with your ancestors. (Zechariah 1:2)

Here in Malachi, God's opening words are completely the opposite: "I have loved you deeply" (1:2).

How tender this is! Like the loving Father that He is, God speaks with great affection for His people. This is the essence of God's character. Yes, He is a God of holiness and judgment who becomes angry when His people sin, but He is also a God of love:

God is love, and all who live in love live in God, and God lives in them. (1 John 4:16)

God is love, but God knows that His people have not loved Him back. In fact, they questioned *how* God has loved them. God responds by telling them that loving them has been His choice. God is the one who loves, and He does it by His own will. God doesn't love us because we first loved Him; we love because He first loved us (1 John 4:19).

The Problem

Despite God's unconditional love, faithfulness, and mercy, we treat Him with indifference; or worse, with disrespect and contempt. The Lord says as much to the people: "You have despised my name!" (1:6).

"But how?" we ask. "How have we despised your name?"

God is quick to answer, but keep in mind that God is not addressing the pagans who have no regard for God in the first place. They're supposed to despise God. Here God is talking to His people, who sacrificed blind, crippled, and diseased animals to God instead of their very best livestock. "'Try giving gifts like that to your governor, and see how pleased he is!' says the LORD Almighty" (1:8).

God is also talking to us. When we worship God apathetically, without knowledge of who He is, it's as if we are giving Him blind animals. When we are careless and inconsistent about serving God, our sacrifices are lame. And when we put our own interests before

God's interests, it's as if we are bringing Him sick animals. Would we dare treat a high-ranking official or a media star with such contempt and disrespect? Yet that's how we treat God.

Truthfully, we dishonor God anytime we don't honor Him with our words and our actions (1:12). Not only are our actions lame, but also our excuses.

> You say, "It's too hard to serve the LORD," and you turn up your noses at his commands. (1:13)

"Hogwash!" God says. (Actually, He doesn't, but our paraphrase is close.) "It would be better for you to do nothing than to promise me your best and then cheat on me with your time and resources."

The Solution

If we've learned anything through this little study of the Minor Prophets, it's that our God is a forgiving God. He is always willing to take us back if we simply turn back to Him. In just a few verses in Malachi 2, God gives us four ways to honor His name:

Give God respect. God calls it *reverence* (2:5). David wrote:

> Reverence for the LORD is the foundation of true wisdom. The rewards of wisdom come to all who obey him. (Psalm 111:10)

Commit to the truth of God's Word. God wants us to pass on to others "all the truth" we receive from him (2:6). The way God gives us His truth is through the Bible:

> All Scripture is inspired by God and is useful to teach us what is true and to make us realize what is wrong in our lives. (2 Timothy 3:16)

Develop Godlike character. This has both a negative and a positive aspect to it. First, don't lie or cheat. Second, walk with God, living a "good and righteous" life (2:6).

Guard the truth. Remember Jack Nicholson's line in *A Few Good Men*? "You can't handle the truth!" Be a person who knows the truth about God. God expected the priests in Malachi's day to "guard knowledge" (2:7). As priests today (that is, people set apart by God for His purposes), we need to be ready to correctly handle the truth:

> Work hard so God can approve you. Be a good worker, one who does not need to be ashamed and who correctly explains the word of truth. (2 Timothy 2:15)

How We Treat One Another

Someone once said that Christians are the only people who shoot their own wounded. When a fellow believer stumbles because of sin, it's like blood in the water and the other believers are sharks. Now, we don't attack our wounded brothers and sisters with our lips curled back so everyone can see our teeth. We're much more subtle. We put out the news on the prayer chain; only we include details that have nothing to do with prayer. "Isn't it a shame about so-and-so?" we say to a friend in the line at Starbucks. Then we share all the lurid tidbits, even if we don't know the whole story.

The New Testament is full of warnings about such inexcusable behavior:

> But I don't need to write to you about the Christian love that should be shown among God's people. For God himself has taught you to love one another. (1 Thessalonians 4:9)

> If someone says, "I love God," but hates a Christian brother or sister, that person is a liar; for if we don't love people we can see, how can we love God, whom we have not seen? (1 John 4:20)

The Problem

Malachi echoes this same condition: When we treat one another poorly, it reflects on our relationships with God. If we say we are children of God, then we need to show it:

Are we not all children of the same Father? Are we not all cre-ated by the same God? Then why are we faithless to each other, violating the covenant of our ancestors? (2:10)

H. A. Ironside observed this about the people of Israel. The same description could be applied to us as well:

The feeble remnant, returned to the land of God's name and separated from the nations, surely needed the strength that comes from unity and mutual love, and brotherly encourage-ment. Outside, the wolves raged and snarled. Inside, the sheep were biting and devouring one another! It's a pitiful picture.[2]

Malachi doesn't stop with our relationships with fellow believers. He goes on to deal with a subject that was as delicate back then as it is today: divorce. Now, we want to be clear that God doesn't con-demn the people who divorce any more than he condemns any of us for all the other things we do that displease Him. God is simply expressing His opinion. (Of course, this *is* God's opinion, so it should carry some weight.)

In a word, God hates divorce (2:16). What's striking about this comment is that it's rare. "The Bible teaches that God hates sin," wrote Boice, "but it rarely says that about a particular sin."[3] So why does God get so worked up about such a specific—and common— problem? Boice gives three reasons.

First, God hates divorce "because it breaks faith, because it vio-lates truth's standard." Second, divorce is harmful, both to the couple involved and also to the extended family, especially the children. Third, God designed the marriage union to illustrate the love that Christ has for us. We are the bride of Christ, and He is the bride-groom. Imagine how God feels when His children separate, espe-cially since He is the one who joined them together. Jesus said:

Since they are no longer two but one, let no one separate them, for God has joined them together. (Matthew 19:6)

Jesus goes on to say that while divorce is permitted, "it was not what God had originally intended" (Matthew 19:8). With God's help and God's blessing, our marriages need to be examples of Christ's love for us. Anything less than that is not God's ideal.

The Solution

This may seem like an overly simple solution, but there's really no way we can complicate it. Whether we are relating to a fellow believer or to our spouses, we need to start with a unity made possible by love. Jesus explained it this way:

> So now I am giving you a new commandment: Love each other. Just as I have loved you, you should love each other. Your love for one another will prove to the world that you are my disciples. (John 13:34–35)

This isn't self-serving love. This is the kind of sacrificial love that Paul described in the famous love chapter:

> Love never gives up, never loses faith, is always hopeful, and endures through every circumstance. (1 Corinthians 13:7)

This is the kind of love that will prove to the world that we are His followers, and that He is the one who loves us with an everlasting love.

"I Am the Lord, and I Do Not Change."

One of the central characteristics of God's personality is His immutability. That's a technical term that means He does not change, and He says it right here in Malachi (3:6). This is an incredibly important truth for us to know about God, because it means we can trust Him to be the same yesterday, today, and forever (Hebrews 13:8). God is always holy, always just, and always loving. His supreme power is constant, and His total knowledge never fails. God never weakens. He isn't susceptible to Alzheimer's.

One of the most important aspects of God's immutability—especially in light of our own tendency to change like the wind—is His

changeless mercy. Just as we can count on the sun to rise every morning, we know that God's mercies "begin afresh each day" (Lamentations
3:23). God's constant mercy, faithfulness, and forgiveness are why He
doesn't just get rid of us for good when we betray Him for the
umpteenth time. They are why He takes us back every time we wander away and then return home again.

How We Treat Our Money

OK, now God's getting personal. It's one thing for Him to criticize the
way we treat Him; He's got a right to be offended for our attitudes of
indifference and disrespect. As for the way we treat other people,
well, that's a problem too. But now God's messing with our money,
and that's just not right.

Right there in Malachi God accuses us of cheating Him out of the
money we owe Him (3:8). What's that all about? Doesn't God own
the cattle on a thousand hills and the gold in every mine? Are we
supposed to relate to God like some celestial creditor? Does God
really need our money?

Yes, He does. But He doesn't need it because He's broke or because
He needs financing to develop Heaven's Mansions: Phase III. This is
God we're talking about here. Material things mean nothing to Him,
but they mean everything to us—and that's the problem.

The Problem

The song may say, "Love makes the world go 'round," but that's
not really true. What turns the world is money. You don't hear people
talk about "global charity." It's always the "global economy." Whether
you're talking dollars, marks, francs, or yen, cash is king.

Jesus understood this all too well. Once a rich young man
approached Him and asked, "Teacher, what good things must I do to
have eternal life?" (Matthew 19:16). This guy had all the material
success life could offer. He wore the latest Armani robes and Gucci
sandals and enjoyed life to the fullest. There was only one problem:
He was secure in this life, but he didn't know about eternal life (his
retirement plan didn't cover the hereafter).

Like a lot of successful people, the rich young guy thought he was living an honorable life before God and men. "I've obeyed all these commandments," he told Jesus. And maybe he had done a pretty good job with the Ten Commandments. But then he asked, "What else must I do?" That's the opening Jesus was looking for.

Because Jesus was God in human form, He possessed all of God's qualities. He knew everything about this man because He knew everything about the human heart. Jesus knew that right there at the center is a love for money that controls us in ways few of us understand or acknowledge. So Jesus looked the rich young man squarely in the eye and said, "If you want to be perfect, go and sell all you have and give the money to the poor, and you will have treasure in heaven. Then come, follow Me."

You've got to be kidding. Certainly God doesn't expect us to sell everything and give the money away, does He? How are we going to live? What about the Volvo Cross Country and the club membership? OK, maybe we don't need the summer home, but does God need our annual ski vacations to Vail? Evidently this was what the rich young guy thought, because the Bible says, "But when the young man heard this, he went sadly away because he had many possessions."

The Solution

Before you break into a cold sweat, you need to know that God doesn't need our cars or our homes or even our cash. What He needs is our hearts. It's always been about the heart, the seat of our emotions and the center of our desires. Because our desires are so often tied to material things, it's impossible for us to separate our hearts from those material things we value. "Wherever your treasure is, there your heart and thoughts will also be" (Luke 12:34).

That's why God has asked us to do something very specific when it comes to our possessions. He wants us to "sell" them to Him, every last one. God wants us to understand that He owns everything in the first place, that everything we have or could ever hope to have comes out of His loving favor. In reality, when we give to God, we are simply returning to Him that which He already owns.

Malachi talked about "tithes and offerings." That seems like such churchy terminology. In fact, tithing is an Old Testament concept based on giving God a tenth of everything the people earned or produced. The tithe was intended for temple service and other social obligations. The people of Israel had not given God the entire tithe. They had kept back a portion for themselves, and this ticked God off. "You have cheated me!" He said.

Officially, the practice of tithing was not carried over into the New Testament, but that doesn't mean we're off the hook. If anything, we need to give more because we have more. The Bible instructs us to set aside "some amount of money" each week in relation to our income and give it to God's work (1 Corinthians 16:2), and it would be hard to argue that we should give less than ten percent of what the Lord has allowed us to earn. But we should never be satisfied with giving God just a portion, no matter how large.

God wants all of us, and that includes all of our money and all of our possessions. He wants us to trust Him completely to take care of us. It's not a money issue; it's a faith issue.

> Can God take care of us? Can God care for His people and at the same time use their willing generosity to provide for Christian work here and in other lands? Of course, He can! To doubt Him in this and give little (in some cases, nothing) is to rob God and slander His sovereignty.
>
> —James Montgomery Boice

Give It a Try

It's no coincidence that some of God's final words in the Old Testament concern money. If we can get this priority straightened out, all kinds of good things will follow. God actually issued a challenge to the people of Israel, and He does the same for us:

> "Bring all the tithes into the storehouse so there will be enough food in my Temple. If you do," says the LORD Almighty, "I will open the windows of heaven for you. I will pour out a blessing so great you won't have enough room to take it in! Try it! Let me prove it to you!" (Malachi 3:10)

A Special Treasure

Are you willing to invest your treasure in heaven? Will you turn your heart toward God and take Him seriously? If so, blessings beyond your imagination are waiting for you. Let these words from Malachi encourage you:

> Then those who feared the LORD spoke with each other, and the LORD listened to what they said. In his presence, a scroll of remembrance was written to record the names of those who feared him and loved to think about him. "They will be my people," says the LORD Almighty. "On the day when I act, they will be my own special treasure. I will spare them as a father spares an obedient and dutiful child. Then you will again see the difference between the righteous and the wicked, between those who serve God and those who do not. (3:16–18)

This entire book has been about those things that tick God off. But we hope you have read between the lines into the heart of God to see that He would much rather bless us than correct us. Make no mistake about it: God *will* correct us when we get off track, but it's only to get us back on the road to blessing. And the greatest blessing is to be called God's people. There's no greater honor.

Our Greatest Hope

Little did people realize that as Malachi gave the last few words of his message, God was about to close the windows of heaven. For the next four hundred years He would be silent. For hundreds of years God had patiently spoken directly to His people through His faithful prophets. Despite warnings of judgment and promises of blessing, many failed to act on God's message. Now, in the closing verses of the Old Testament record, God wants to make something very clear:

> The day of judgment is coming, burning like a furnace. The arrogant and the wicked will be burned up like straw on that day. They will be consumed like a tree—roots and all. (4:1)

That's a gloomy picture that should make us shudder. But it doesn't have to be our fate. For those who take God seriously and do what He says, there is an entirely different scenario:

> But for you who fear my name, the Sun of Righteousness will
> rise with healing in his wings. (4:2)

And who is the Sun of Righteousness? It's Jesus Christ, the light of the world, who would be born just as the prophets predicted. "Life itself was in him," wrote John, "and this life gives light to everyone. The light shines through the darkness, and the darkness can never extinguish it" (John 1:4–5).

Jesus said, "I am the light of the world. If you follow me, you won't be stumbling through the darkness, because you will have the light that leads to life" (John 8:12). Peter said, "There is no other name in all of heaven for people to call on to save them" (Acts 4:12). God has no other plan to heal the sin sickness of this world.

As the book of Malachi closed, so did the Old Testament. God may have been silent, but He was working to prepare the world for the coming of His Son into the world. He was moving heaven and earth to get things ready. When everything was right, Jesus was born. No longer would God need to speak through prophets. From that day forward, God spoke through Jesus:

> Long ago God spoke many times and in many ways to our
> ancestors through the prophets. But now in these final days,
> he has spoken to us through his Son. (Hebrews 1:1–2)

God is still working, and God is still preparing the world for the coming of His Son into the world a second time, to take His people to that place He has prepared for those who have put their faith in Him. That is our greatest hope.

> Because of our faith, Christ has brought us into this place of
> highest privilege where we now stand, and we confidently and
> joyfully look forward to sharing God's glory. (Romans 5:2)

NOTES

Chapter 2

1. Eugene Peterson, *A Long Obedience in the Same Direction* (Downers Grove, Ill: Intervarsity Press, 1980), 25.
2. James Montgomery Boice, *The Minor Prophets* (Grand Rapids, Mich.: Kregel Publications, 1996), 117.
3. Erwin Lutzer, *Ten Lies about God* (Nashville: Word Publishing, 2000), 117.

Chapter 3

1. *A Christmas Carol*, Entertainment Partners, New York, 1984.

Chapter 4

1. Boice, *The Minor Prophets*, 191.
2. Ibid., 192.
3. Kay Arthur, *The International Inductive Study Bible* (Eugene, Oreg.: Harvest House Publishers, 1993), 1479.

Chapter 8

1. John Phillips, *Ironside Commentaries, Introductory Notes* (Neptune, N.J.: Loizeaux, 1999), 209.
2. C. S. Lewis, *The Problem of Pain* (New York: The Macmillan Company, 1970), 89.
3. Ibid., 69.
4. Norman Geisler and Ron Brooks, *When Skeptics Ask* (Grand Rapids, Mich.: Baker Books, 1990), 63.
5. Philip Yancey, *Where Is God When It Hurts?* (Grand Rapids, Mich.: Zondervan Publishing House, 1990), 68.
6. Ibid., 82.
7. Ibid., 83–84.
8. Lewis, 96.
9. Ibid., 110.
10. Phillips, *Ironside Commentaries*, 210.

Chapter 10

1. Feinberg, *The Minor Prophets*, 238.
2. Ibid., 242.

Chapter 12

1. Matthew Henry, *Matthew Henry's Concise Commentary on the Whole Bible* (Nashville: Thomas Nelson, Inc., 1997), 833.
2. H. A. Ironside, *Minor Prophets* (Neptune, N.J.: Loizeaux, 1999), 333.
3. Boice, *The Minor Prophets*, 245.